BURGER
OF THE DAY

THE
BOB'S BURGERS
BURGER BOOK

REAL RECIPES FOR JOKE BURGERS

LOREN BOUCHARD
AND THE WRITERS OF BOB'S BURGERS

RECIPES BY COLE BOWDEN

HYPERION
AVENUE

LOS ANGELES · NEW YORK

BURGERS OF THE DAY

A LONG BURGER OF THE DAY'S JOURNEY INTO A COOK BOOK

When we decided there would be a Burger of the Day chalkboard behind the counter in Bob's Burgers, mostly what we wanted you to think was "Poor Bob—it's just so easy for his rascally nine year old daughter to climb up there and change the burger name to something undesirable." That was how "The Child Molester (comes with candy)" made it into our pilot episode. (And by the way, we're not, like, *proud* of that joke. That's not the joke burger that you put on a T-shirt.) But we moved away from the burger-as-prank pretty quickly after that. And it had nothing to do with the fact that it would double the number of burger puns we'd have to write every episode. Nothing.

Rather than a running joke about the easy erasability of chalk, the Burger of the Day board came to be sort of a smudgy little window *into* Bob himself—Bob, the restless creator of new tastes and bad puns. Every single day, we imagine, this ambitious grill cook tasks himself with the creation of a new burger special and a silly name for it. *Occasionally* clever, more often sweaty, and typically related to what's happening in his life at that time, the names Bob gives his Burgers of the Day are supposed to feel not just like a free joke glimpsed in the background of an animated show but also—and this is going to sound grandiose and gross, sorry—an expression of the internal life of the character (there, I said it) and also offer a hint that this greasy little mom and pop shop might be more gastronomically adventurous than it would otherwise appear to be. That Bob is something of a sweaty, greasy ground beef auteur, laboring over his grill like a wild-haired artist, questing after burger perfection, that despite his tragically struggling business, his burgers are supposed to be *really* good.

But *are* they? I mean, would they be, if they were real? They're jokes—puns dreamt up by writers on a deadline. If you actually made them—forget *good*—would they even be edible? We reject the ones that sound like they're all joke and no burger, like "The America's Toast Wanted Burger (comes on a toasted bun)" or the ones that sound good but whose names are too mean or too risqué—the "Child Molester" aside—like "The Young, Dumb, and Full of Plum Burger." So, in other words, we *sort of* make an effort to create palatable burgers with our somewhat palatable puns. But all we can do, really, is *hope* that they'd taste good if they existed in real life.

But then there came a blog— a beautiful fan burger blog called The Bob's Burger Experiment. This brave soul, a young man named Cole Bowden, was making each and every burger that appeared on our show's chalkboard and he was writing about it. It was as if we had dreamt him up—conjured him from the wilds of the blogosphere in order to legitimize us—to add a dash of respectability to our made-up food.

For those of us who worked on the show and followed him, Cole's culinary ambition was thrilling, and his chutzpah and hard work was and is inspiring to say the least, but when you read his recipes it becomes clear that primarily what he brings to the table is *imagination*. Cole approaches each Burger of the Day as an intrepid interpreter, like a jazz musician improvising around a tune. He's a culinary Miles Davis, if Miles Davis also had a blog.

Could he have, in a fit of exuberance, combined flavors that might usually be left on opposite sides of the plate? Of course. And he makes no claim otherwise. He is a passionate amateur, a pioneer, testing his theories and reporting on the results. So, for the purposes of making the best possible cookbook, we invited two working chefs—Aliza Miner in Los Angeles, and Paul O'Connell in Boston—to read Cole's recipes and consult. These two experienced cooks took on the role of culinary big sister and brother, poking, prodding, and giving noogies to Cole's recipes in the interest of bringing them to their full potential.

We want you to make these burgers. We want you to adjust and play with these burgers. We want you to befriend these burgers and then build a life with them. There are many people, including professionals who should know better, who will tell you that all burgers should be "classic." But these classicists are dangerously conservative. Pay them no mind! How would we have found even the simple cheeseburger, or the bacon burger, if it weren't for people fooling around with toppings? How about ketchup, or lettuce, or tomato? Or buns?

Restaurants can ban ketchup if that's how they want to present their food (Sidebar: isn't ketchup delicious? It's the best, right?), but that's not Bob's Burgers. And that's not this book. Our approach is, in fact, the opposite. We want you to put all kinds of crap on your burger. We want you to approach burgers the way that Cole does and how we imagine that Bob does, which is in the spirit of brave, even fool-hardy experimentation, because only by this process will our science advance. And maybe someday, we'll all wonder why we didn't always eat "Free to Brie You and Me" burgers or "Home for the Challah-Days" burgers. Classics, we'll call them. But you made them here first.

HOW TO COOK A BASIC BURGER BEST

Anyone can throw a bunch of ground beef on a grill and call it a burger. But does that make it a *good* burger? Does throwing a habit on a dog make it a good nun? No. Follow these steps for the meat-based burger recipes in this book and you'll be on the path to burger perfection, which we call burg-fection.

First, start with cold, high quality, freshly ground "choice" grade chuck, and use a kitchen scale to measure it out. If you don't have a kitchen scale, congratulations, you're a normal person. If you have a 1-lb package then it's easy: divide into 4 equal portions and you've got quarter-pound burgers. Want a big, honkin' 1/3-lb patty? Well, that sounds big. Are you sure? Okay. Divide your package in thirds. Did you buy more than a pound of ground beef? Then you know what? Just tear off a ball about the size of your fist.

For most burgers, 80% lean ground beef is as lean as you want to go. Fat is flavor! And whoever says otherwise is probably just freaking out about fat and isn't listening to what you said. Feel free to ask your butcher for 70%. They can actually add fat to 80% lean chuck while they're grinding.

Use clean hands and don't play with the meat. This includes making meat animals or any kind of meat creature. It will be tempting, but resist! Kneading the meat too much will give your burgers a chewy texture. If mixing other ingredients such as cheese or spice into your ground beef, do so gently and just to combine—the show's not called *Bob's Meatloaf*.

Burgers shrink when you cook them so **form your patties a little larger than your buns** (your burger buns). To get flat burgers, use your thumbs to form a shallow indent in the middle of the patty. When the burgers bulge up during cooking, they'll still end up flat.

Plain ground beef is actually boring. Sorry, ground beef, but it's true. You're going to have to season the patties right before they hit the pan or grill. **This means liberally dusting them on both sides with salt and fresh cracked pepper.** Start with about 1 teaspoon of salt and almost as much pepper per 1 pound of beef and adjust to your taste. Remember: You can cook a burger naked, but you should never cook a naked burger.

Cooking burgers on the grill has a certain *paleo* appeal, and it is unquestionably the smell and the taste of summer, so if you're in the mood, fire it up, but you should know that most professionals use a flat top, and you have a flat top in your house—it's called a frying pan. **When you cook in a pan, more of the fat and moisture stay in the burger.** You also get more surface contact, which means more caramelization, which means more flavor. Melt a pat of butter in your pan before you add the meat or use cooking oil.

The USDA recommends that you cook your burger until the middle is 160ºF because E. coli is only effectively killed at 155 and above. Ignore these guidelines and your last words may be "USDA, my ass." Get a cheap food thermometer or get the expensive instant-read kind but get one.

Grill or cook a good sized patty for about 4 or 5 minutes per side and then stick the thermometer in from the edge, all the way to the center. Keep cooking until you get a reading just under the USDA recommended temperature (it will continue to cook after it's removed from the heat—this is called carry-over cooking). You'll wind up with a reliable time estimate that will be somewhere between be 4 and 8 minutes per side and you'll learn what a well-cooked burger looks and feels like using your chosen method. And that higher fat content in your beef? That helps you here—you'll get a nice, juicy burger even at USDA-approved temperatures. Leaner meat will dry out faster.

If you're making cheeseburgers—and honestly, why wouldn't you?—**add your cheese to the patties after you flip them.** Cover the pan or grill, or tent the patties with foil to help the cheese melt and just generally feel cozy.

Let your burgers rest for a minute or two after cooking. This allows the juices to redistribute into the meat. While your patties are resting, lightly toast your buns (your burger buns).

Speaking of buns, these puffy pillows of bread are the last great frontier of burger research. **Seek out freshly baked buns whenever possible.** Brioche-style, Kaiser, sesame– you should try them all. Just like your butcher is waiting to grind beef for you, there are bakers working hard right now to help you make your next burger great. Go to them. Go. Tell them about how we call burger perfection burg-fection. See if they like that. See if they laugh.

HOW TO COOK YOUR OWN FRIES FAULTLESSLY

The French fry is burger's soul mate - the salty side that burger sees across a crowded dance floor and says to itself, "there's the one I've been looking for." **We like russet potatoes and peanut oil.** You can use other potatoes and fry them in lard if you like, but let's start with russet and peanut.

Wash your russets well. No one likes a dirty potato, and that's not a euphemism. **Peeling is optional.** For fancy-looking fries, peel, then cut off the ends and sides of each potato to form a box shape. Cut this box into ¼-inch slices, turn it on its side, then cut ¼-inch slices again. You will end up with long thin potato sticks. Of course you can make shoe string fries with a vegetable slicer, or you can make big ol' fries with skin all over the place. The recipe is more or less the same no matter how you slice 'em. **Place the cut potatoes in ice water for at least five minutes.** This gets rid of excess starch. It also keeps the potatoes focused.

Drain the wet potato sticks, spread on paper towels and *thoroughly* pat dry—you do not want to combine water with hot oil unless you're a fan of sputtering hot oil. **Heat your oil to 325°F in a heavy, high walled pot.** Check the temperature with a frying or candy thermometer. Use enough oil to cover your fries. In batches, drop in the potato sticks and cook for 5 minutes, until limp. Don't cover. Don't let them brown. Remove carefully with a *long handled* slotted spoon or metal strainer and place on paper towels. **Are you being really super duper extra careful?** That's *hot oil* on your stove. Use the back burner. Use controlled movements. Later, after dinner, you can start swinging your arms and legs around wildly, but not right now. After the blanched potato sticks have cooled to room temperature, bring the oil up to 375°F. In small batches, **drop the blanched sticks back into the oil for about 3 more minutes**, or until golden brown. Remove from pot and drain on paper towels. Again, keep your oil temperature steady, and keep the hot oil off of humans. You can't really call them "faultless fries" if you or someone you love has a third degree burn.

Toss the fries in a large bowl with salt and you're done. 'Course, you can also fool around with black pepper, rosemary, chili powder, garlic salt, onion salt, or paprika. But you don't want the fries to be like, hey, look at me, look at me! Burgers and fries are soul mates because they support each other. So season appropriately.

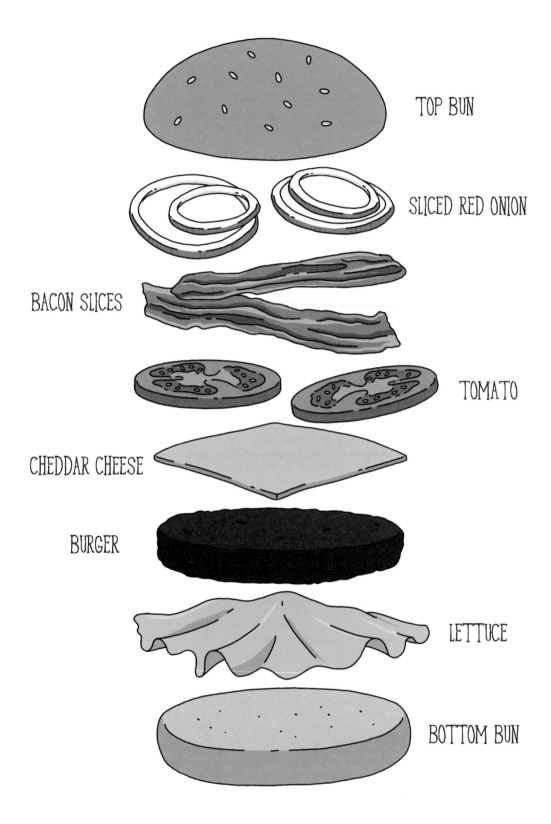

TOP BUN

SLICED RED ONION

BACON SLICES

TOMATO

CHEDDAR CHEESE

BURGER

LETTUCE

BOTTOM BUN

NEW BACON-INGS BURGER

SEASON 1, EPISODE 1: HUMAN FLESH

A classic all-beef patty topped with lettuce, cheddar cheese, onion, tomato, and bacon. It's what George Washington was fighting for. It's what the Statue of Liberty wishes it was holding instead of a dumb torch. So use the freshest ingredients you can find, down to the bun. MAKES 4 BURGERS, PLUS PLENTY OF FRIES

1 pound bacon

French fries, page 9

1 pound ground beef

1 cup whole milk

1 large egg

4 buns

Green leaf lettuce

1 large tomato, sliced

1 red onion, sliced

1 Preheat your oven to 400°F. If you prefer to cook your bacon in a skillet, chop all but 8 slices and fry over medium heat until almost crisp and most of the fat has rendered. Drain the chopped bacon on paper towels, wipe out the skillet, and fry the remaining slices till crisp. Drain and reserve. Or, spread the strips onto a rack placed in a rimmed baking sheet and bake in the oven until brown and crisp, about 15 to 20 minutes. Reserve 8 slices and finely chop the rest. Keep the oven on.

2 Following the steps on page 9, cook your French fries through the blanching stage but do not deep-fry. Drain and let cool.

3 Combine the milk and egg in a large bowl. Coat the blanched, cooled fries in the mixture and spread on a parchment-lined backing sheet. Toss the coated fries with the chopped bacon and return to the oven for 10 to 15 minutes, until the bacon-y fries are extra crispy.

4 Meanwhile, make 4 patties, season both sides with salt and pepper, and cook your burgers. When they're just about done, top with the cheese.

5 BUILD YOUR BURGER: Bottom bun, lettuce, cheeseburger, tomato, bacon slices, onion, top bun. Serve with bacon-y fries.

EGGERS CAN'T BE CHEESERS BURGER

SEASON 3, EPISODE 11: NUDE BEACH

An all-beef patty topped with American cheese and a fried egg sunny-side up. Served with hot sauce and a piece of lettuce on a plain bun. It's eggsactly as eggstraordinary as it sounds. **Eggs.** MAKES 4 BURGERS

---

1 pound ground beef

8 slices American cheese

4 large eggs

Butter

4 English muffins

Green leaf lettuce

Hot sauce (optional, but better)

---

1 Make 4 patties, season both sides with salt and pepper, and cook the burgers. When they're just about done, top with the cheese (2 slices per burger). Cover the pan if you're cooking inside to help melt the cheese.

2 In a large frying pan, cook your eggs sunny-side up over a bit of butter. No flipping these guys—that's what sunny side up means. It's also a good way to describe your attitude these days.

3 Toast your English muffins.

4 BUILD YOUR BURGER: Spread a tiny bit of butter on your toasted English muffins, then bottom muffin, cheeseburger, and egg on top. Finish it with a dash of hot sauce, and the muffin top. YOUR muffin top is gonna love it!

5 Grab a napkin—you'll need it!

A GOOD MANCHEGO IS HARD TO FIND BURGER

SEASON 5, EPISODE 10: LATE AFTERNOON IN THE GARDEN OF BOB AND LOUISE

A burger topped with caramelized shallots, Manchego cheese, and a generous helping of fig jam. Fig jam! Banned. Banned!! Remember? From the show?

MAKES 4 BURGERS

2 tablespoons butter

6 shallots, peeled and thinly sliced

1 pound ground beef

1 small block Manchego cheese, sliced

Fig jam

4 buns

Arugula or Boston lettuce

1 Melt the butter in a wide frying pan over medium-low heat. Add the shallots and stir to coat. Cook over fairly low heat, stirring occasionally, until the shallots are very soft and a deep, sticky golden-brown, about 15 to 20 minutes.

2 Form 4 patties, season both sides with salt and pepper, and cook the burgers, melting a few slices of Manchego over each burger. Cover the pan or tent with foil to help the cheese melt.

3 BUILD YOUR BURGER: Bottom bun, then the cheeseburger, arugula, and sautéed shallots. Spread the fig jam on the top bun. Spread happiness in your face.

TOTALLY RADISH BURGER

SEASON 1, EPISODE 5: HAMBURGER DINNER THEATER

An all-beef patty topped with a refreshingly crunchy-creamy-spicy mix of crème fraîche, cucumbers, dill, and radishes. Slice any leftover radishes for a fancy garnish. Your friends will say "Hey, nice garnish." MAKES 4 BURGERS

---

1 cucumber, peeled

About 10–12 radishes

⅓ cup crème fraîche

1 tablespoon chopped fresh dill

1 pound ground beef

Green leaf lettuce

4 French rolls (plain buns are fine, too)

---

1 Use a microplane to grate the cucumber and the radishes into a medium bowl. Add the crème fraîche and the dill and mix.

2 Form 4 patties, season both sides with salt and pepper, and cook your burgers.

3 BUILD YOUR BURGER: Put some lettuce and a burger on the bottom roll, some of that delicious radish-cucumber mixture, top bun.

4 Add the garnish. Did you forget? We *just* talked about it. You know what, it's fine. I don't know why I'm making such a big deal about it.

POBLANO PICASSO BURGER

SEASON 1, EPISODE 8: ART CRAWL

An all-beef patty topped with a spicy poblano salsa verde, fresh tomatoes, and Monterey Jack cheese. A Picasso never tasted so good. I mean, we're assuming his paintings tasted terrible. Anyway, this burger is delicious.

MAKES 4 BURGERS

¼ cup chopped white onions

1 teaspoon butter

1 large poblano pepper, stemmed, halved lengthwise, and seeded

4 tomatillos, husked and quartered

1 jalapeño pepper

1 pound ground beef

4 slices Monterey Jack cheese

4 buns

Green leaf lettuce

1 large tomato, thickly sliced

---

1 Preheat your broiler.

2 Cook the onions in a small frying pan with butter over medium-high heat until translucent.

3 Put the poblano and tomatillos in a small casserole dish and place 6 inches under the broiler for 5 to 10 minutes, until the skins start to brown.

4 Add the cooked onions, broiled poblano and tomatillos, and the jalapeño to a food processor or blender, and puree; set aside.

5 Form 4 patties, season both sides with salt and pepper, and cook the burgers as you normally would, making sure to melt a heavy helping of Monterey Jack on top.

6 BUILD YOUR BURGER: Bottom bun, cheeseburger, a generous helping of salsa verde, tomato, and the top bun. You're poblano-ly gonna love this one. Get it? Like probably?

DO THE BRUSSEL BURGER

SEASON 2, EPISODE 3: SYNCHRONIZED SWIMMING

Brussels sprouts. As kids, we hid them in potted plants close so we wouldn't have to eat them, and as adults, we love 'em. Life's funny, isn't it? This lightly seasoned bacon burger topped with sautéed sprouts and pistachios will have you "doin' the brussel" right at the table. MAKES 4 BURGERS

½ pound bacon

⅓ pound Brussels sprouts, thinly sliced

¼ cup shelled pistachios, roughly chopped

1 pound ground beef

4 buns

Green leaf lettuce

Sour cream

---

1 Cook your bacon on the stove in a large frying pan set over low heat. Cook the bacon until it's crispy, but not too crispy.

2 Transfer your bacon to paper towels, and throw your Brussels sprouts into that delicious bacon fat; increase the heat to medium-high. You could cook garden tools in bacon fat and they would taste good. That's a fact!**

3 Once the sprouts start to brown a bit, add the pistachios. Stir for about a minute, then remove from heat and set aside.

4 Season the beef with the salt and pepper, form 4 patties, and cook your burgers in the same pan.

5 BUILD YOUR BURGER: Bottom bun, burger, bacon, Brussels sprouts mixture, a dollop of sour cream, and your top bun. Dollop. Dollop. That's a great word, dollop.

** Don't eat garden tools

IT'S FUN TO EAT AT THE RYE-MCA BURGER

SEASON 2, EPISODE 6: DR. YAP

All-beef patties on rye bread topped with cheddar cheese, brown mustard, caramelized onions and horseradish. Or, if you're a stickler for episode accuracy, you can substitute sliced avocado for the horseradish. MAKES 4 BURGERS

---

1 tablespoon butter

½ medium onion, sliced

1 pound ground beef

Thickly sliced cheddar cheese, up to ¼-inch thick

Sliced rye bread (Don't skimp here, get the good stuff from a bakery—there's nothing worse than discount rye bread.)

Boston or green leaf lettuce

4 teaspoons prepared horse-radish (or 1 avocado, sliced)

Brown mustard

Cook the Onions

1 Melt the butter in a wide frying pan over medium-low heat. Add the onion and stir to coat. Cook over low heat, stirring occasionally, until the onions are soft and a sticky golden-brown, about 20 to 30 minutes.

Make the Burgers

1 Make patties, season both sides with salt and pepper, and cook them as you normally would. Just before they finish cooking, lay a thick slice of cheddar cheese over each patty, and cover or tent to help the cheese melt.

2 BUILD YOUR BURGER: Rye bread, lettuce, cheeseburger, caramelized onions, a spoonful of horseradish (or a couple slices of avocado), and another piece of rye bread with brown mustard slathered all over it. Tastes best when eaten with a cowboy, a police officer, a Native American, a construction worker, someone in leather, and an army guy.

IF LOOKS COULD KALE BURGER

SEASON 2, EPISODE 7: MOODY FOODIE

This all-beef patty is topped with deliciously complex Gruyère cheese and crispy roasted kale. Serve on a toasted whole wheat bun with a side of rosemary orzo salad. This burger gives you instant kale-bragging rights—you jumped on the kale train and you're riding it all the way to flavor town.

MAKES 4 BURGERS

---

3 1/4 cups low-sodium chicken stock

2 cups orzo

1/3 cup diced tomatoes

2 sprigs fresh rosemary, leaves finely chopped

Olive oil

1 pound ground beef

1 cup grated Gruyère cheese

4 whole wheat or whole grain buns

1 big bunch dark green kale, stems removed and leaves cut into ribbons

4 cloves garlic, minced

Olive oil

2 tablespoons red wine vinegar

Make the Orzo Salad

1 Bring chicken stock to a boil and drop in the orzo. Cook for 10 minutes, stirring occasionally, and then drain. Mix in the tomatoes and rosemary and set aside. Serve orzo hot or cold.

Make the Kale

1 Preheat your oven to 300°F.

2 Wash and dry and the kale. Then "de-stem" it by pulling the leaves off of the stem and shred the leaves into pieces about the size of playing cards.

3 Cover a baking pan with a piece of parchment paper, lay the kale on the paper, brush with olive oil and sprinkle liberally with salt.

4 Bake for 10 minutes, then rotate the pan and bake for approximately another 10 minutes. Watch your kale closely during the last few minutes. You want it crispy but not burnt. Set it aside.

Make the Burgers

1 Form 4 patties, season both sides with salt and pepper, and cook your burgers as you usually would. Cover each burger with Gruyère. Toast your buns. No, not those buns. The burger buns.

2 BUILD YOUR BURGER: Bottom bun, cheeseburger, crispy kale, top bun. It's a burger to relieve whatever kales you. Sorry.

THE FINAL KRAUT DOWN BURGER

SEASON 2, EPISODE 7: MOODY FOODIE

Sweet Bavarian sauerkraut, caramelized onions, Swiss cheese, and burger, served on a Kaiser roll. Bavarian style is a much milder, sweeter style of sauerkraut, so quit fighting it! Give in! Give in to Bavaria! MAKES 4 BURGERS

---

1 tablespoon butter

1 Vidalia onion, chopped

1 14.5-ounce can Bavarian-style sauerkraut, drained and rinsed

1 pound ground beef

Swiss cheese, sliced

4 kaiser rolls

Dijon mustard

---

1 Melt the butter in a wide frying pan over medium-low heat. Add the onion and stir to coat. Cook over fairly low heat, stirring occasionally, until the onions are very soft and a deep, sticky golden-brown, about 20 to 30 minutes. They'll smell amazingly rich and sweet. So will you. I mean, you did already, but now you will even more.

2 Mix the sauerkraut in with the caramelized onions and stir to combine. You're only heating up the sauerkraut. That's all. Nothing to be scared of. You're doing great.

3 MAKE YOUR BURGERS: season the beef with the salt and pepper, form 4 patties, and cook. Melt the cheese on top as you normally would.

4 BUILD YOUR BURGER: Bottom roll, cheeseburger, sauerkraut-onion mixture, mustard, top roll.

BRUSCHETTA BOUT IT BURGER

SEASON 2, EPISODE 9: BEEFSQUATCH

An all-beef patty topped with bruschetta and fresh mozzarella cheese, dressed with balsamic vinegar, and served on toasted French bread. Delicious, easy, and full of bold bright flavors. Just like the mafia! MAKES 4 BURGERS

5 Roma tomatoes, seeded and chopped into ¼-inch cubes

1 clove garlic, minced

1 bunch fresh basil, leaves stacked, rolled, and cut into thin ribbons

2 tablespoons olive oil

1 tablespoon balsamic vinegar

1 pound ground beef

1 ball fresh mozzarella, cut into thick slices

French bread

1 Set the tomatoes, garlic, and basil in a large mixing bowl. Add the olive oil, balsamic vinegar, and a dash of salt and pepper to the bowl and stir to combine. Set aside.

2 Form 4 patties, season both sides with salt and pepper, and cook them. Just before they're cooked to your liking, melt the mozz slices over the burgers. Toast 2 slices of French bread for each burger.

3 BUILD YOUR BURGER: Toasted French bread, cheeseburger, a heavy scoop of the bruschetta, top slice of toasted French bread.

4 Eat it. Think about all you've accomplished. That burger you just made, other stuff... It's been a good day.

SWEATY PALMS BURGER

SEASON 2, EPISODE 8: BAD TINA

An all-beef patty topped with Parmesan and a spicy hearts of palm and artichoke tapenade. It's like a tap(enade) dance in your mouth! Ha cha cha!

MAKES 4 BURGERS

1 pound ground beef

1 cup grated Parmesan cheese

1 14-ounce can sliced hearts of palm, whole or sliced

1 14-ounce can artichoke hearts

2 cloves garlic

10 pitted green olives

8 pitted kalamata olives

1 Serrano chili

About 5 leaves fresh basil

2 tablespoons olive oil

1 tablespoon balsamic vinegar

4 buns

1 Form 4 patties, season both sides with salt and pepper, and cook them as you normally would. Before they finish, pile about ¼ cup of grated Parmesan cheese onto each burger and cover or tent to help it melt.

2 Put everything else (except the buns) into a food processor (or mini chopper) and pulse until the mixture is chunky but spreadable. Then put Chunky But Spreadable on a bumper sticker and watch the money come rolling in.

3 TOAST THE BUNS AND BUILD YOUR BURGER: Bottom bun, cheeseburger, tapenade, top bun.

POUTINE ON THE RITZ BURGER

SEASON 2, EPISODE 9: BEEFSQUATCH

Oh, Canada! This friends-from-the-north-inspired recipe is made up of an all-beef patty topped with fresh cheese curds, brown gravy, and Ritz cracker crumbs. And it comes with a side of poutine fries. It's the kind of meal that makes your heart say, "Why do you hate me?" But it's delicious enough for you to say to your heart, "Deal with it, you baby!" Like a good man, fresh cheese curds may be a bit hard to find, but you can usually get them at higher end grocery stores or local dairies. MAKES 4 BURGERS, PLUS PLENTY OF EXTRA POUTINE FRIES

3 tablespoons black pepper, divided

2 tablespoons paprika

2 teaspoons cayenne pepper

French fries, page 9

4 tablespoons butter

6 tablespoons flour

3 cups beef stock

1 pound ground beef

Salt

4 buns

Fresh cheese curds

1 sleeve Ritz crackers

1 Combine 2 tablespoons of the pepper with the paprika and cayenne in a large bowl. Following the steps on page 9, cook your French fries. Toss the finished fries with the pepper mixture and a pinch of salt and keep warm.

2 To make the gravy, melt the butter in a saucepan over medium heat and then whisk in the flour. Keep whisking until the mix starts to turn a light brown and you can smell the toasty aroma. This is now a roux. Add in 2 cups of the beef stock and stir until completely combined. Stir in remaining 1 tablespoon black pepper, and then slowly add the remaining stock. It's okay to leave some out if you like thicker gravy.

3 Make 4 patties, season both sides with salt and pepper, and cook your burgers.

4 BUILD YOUR BURGER: Bottom bun, burger, a bunch of cheese curds, brown gravy, a gratuitous amount of crumbled Ritz crackers, top bun.

5 For the fries, simply mix in some cheese curds and pour some gravy on top. You can do this with loose change or a bucket of golf balls too, but do not eat—it would just be for fun in that situation.

EVERY BREATH YOU TIKKA MASALA BURGER

SEASON 2, EPISODE 9: BEEFSQUATCH

A delicious Indian-inspired burger topped with masala basmati rice and Thai basil. We suggest lamb. Ground lamb sounds cruel, like something an ogre would eat, but lamb might become your new favorite exotic burger meat. The contrast between the basil and the masala is also delicious. Serve with a side of sweet and spicy potatoes. MAKES 8 BURGERS, PLUS PLENTY OF MASALA POTATOES

---

2 cups basmati rice

3 large potatoes, diced

4 sweet peppers (not bell peppers), finely diced

1 hot chile pepper, seeded and finely diced

2 tablespoons butter

Paprika

1 large onion, coarsely diced

1 clove garlic, minced

2 14.5-ounce cans whole plum tomatoes

1 teaspoon ground cumin

1 teaspoon curry powder

1 teaspoon ground ginger

1 teaspoon salt

1 tablespoon garam masala

1 cup plain yogurt

2 pounds ground beef or lamb

8 buns

Fresh Thai basil leaves (1 cup)

Make the Rice

1 Don't skip this step. Rinse your rice until the water runs clear, then let it soak in clean water for at least 30 minutes.

2 Bring 3½ cups of water to a boil in a large saucepan. Add the rice and stir. Reduce the heat to a simmer and cook, covered, until done (until all the water is absorbed and the rice is moist but not sticking to the pot).

Make the Potatoes

1 Preheat the oven to 200°F. Cover the potatoes in a large saucepan with water and season with salt. Bring the potatoes to a boil, reduce the heat to a simmer, and cook just until tender.

2 In a large ovenproof frying pan, sauté the peppers in a tablespoon of butter until the chili pepper heat hits your eyes and your kitchen smells delicious.

3 Drain the potatoes and add them to the pan with the peppers. Sprinkle with a generous amount of paprika and bake for about 20 to 30 minutes (or until the sauce is done and you're ready to eat).

Make the Masala

1 Sauté the onion over medium-high heat in the remaining tablespoon of butter until translucent. Add the garlic.

2 Add the tomatoes and their juice to the onions and keep the mixture at a simmer. Add in the cumin, curry powder, and ginger. Wait for the tomatoes "to sweat"— that's kind of a fancy cooking term for when they start to release their liquid, you can see the liquid sort of pool up in a lighter color. When this happens, add in the salt and masala.

3 Let the mixture reduce for about ten minutes, and then remove from heat. Give it some time to cool (until you can touch it without burning your finger).

4 Add the yogurt and mix it up. The yogurt will curdle but you didn't ruin anything! You're still a good person and this is totally safe to eat. It just means that the yogurt is in contact with an acid; it's not like curdled milk. Mix enough masala with the rice so that it is saturated but not soupy; reserve remaining masala for the potatoes.

Make the Burgers

1 Form 8 patties, season both sides with salt and pepper, and grill or cook the burgers as you normally would.

2 TOAST THE BUNS, THEN BUILD YOUR BURGER: Bottom buns, burger, masala-rice mixture, basil leaves, top buns.

3 Pour the remaining masala over the potatoes and serve on the side.

TOP BUN

CHÈVRE

SHALLOTS

BURGER

ARUGULA

BOTTOM BUN

HIT ME WITH YOUR BEST SHALLOT BURGER

SEASON 1, EPISODE 10: BURGER WARS

How French can we get? This French! This thyme-seasoned burger is topped with caramelized shallots, has a creamy chèvre spread, and is served on a fresh French bread-style roll. MAKES 4 BURGERS

10 small shallots

3 tablespoons butter

1 tablespoon red wine vinegar

2 sprigs rosemary

2 sprigs sage

1 pound ground beef

1 teaspoon chopped fresh thyme

1 4-ounce log chèvre, room temperature

4 French rolls

Arugula

1 This is a garlic peeling technique that works for shallots too: Put your shallots in a bowl and cover them with boiling water. Let them sit for about 10 minutes. Remove from the water, cut the root end off, peel them, and then slice into slivers.

2 In a frying pan, melt the butter over medium heat. Put your shallots in, along with the rosemary and sage. Cook, stirring once in a while, until the shallots are dark brown. Stir in the red wine vinegar at this point. Remove the shallots and set aside, leaving any liquid in the pan.

3 Form 4 patties and season both sides with the fresh thyme, salt, and pepper. Cook your patties in the pan you used for your shallots.

4 SPREAD SOME CHÈVRE ON YOUR TOP BUN, AND BUILD YOUR BURGER: Bottom bun, arugula, burger, a couple of shallots, top bun. "Best shallot?" More like new best friend, right?

I'VE CREATED A MUENSTER BURGER

SEASON 1, EPISODE 11: WEEKEND AT MORT'S

Perfect patties topped with sautéed mushrooms and smothered in muenster cheese, with a dollop of ketchup and lettuce for a bit of color. Muenster is a pretty subtle cheese, but it adds a lot of texture to this burger. (Muenster also happens to be number four on Gene's "Cheeses That Please Me" list. Check often, he updates that list frequently.) MAKES 4 BURGERS

---

1 10-ounce package white button mushrooms, sliced. (Verify that the mushrooms are, in fact, cute as a button.)

2 tablespoons butter

1 pound ground beef

8 thick slices muenster cheese

4 buns

Green leaf or Boston lettuce (if using Boston lettuce, consider renaming this the "Green Muenster Burger," but only if you plan on serving it to someone from Boston because only they will get it)

Ketchup

---

1 Sauté the mushrooms in the butter over medium-high heat until they are limp and light brown.

2 Form 4 patties and season both sides with salt and pepper. Cook the burgers.

3 While the burgers are over the heat, put one slice of Muenster on each burger. Then pile on a healthy scoop of mushrooms and then a second slice of Muenster to hold the mushrooms in place.

4 BUILD YOUR BURGER: Bottom bun, lettuce and a cheesy mushroomy burger, a dash of ketchup to taste, top bun.

THE JACK-O'-LENTIL BURGER

SEASON 3, EPISODE 2: FULL BARS

An all-beef patty topped with a mixture of orange lentils, serrano chiles, garlic, and onions. A light spread of herb-coated chèvre cheese and some fresh spinach finish it off with a rich, over-the-top flavor. We're talking about Over the Top, the movie—this hamburger tastes like arm wrestling. Adding ginger, honey, garlic, serrano chiles, and onions makes the lentils come alive with flavor (once the lentils come to life, you must feed them three times a day). MAKES 4 BURGERS

---

1 cup dried orange lentils

5 cloves garlic, minced

½ green bell pepper, diced

2 celery stalks, finely diced

½ onion, diced

3 serrano chiles, seeded and finely diced

Olive oil

1 tablespoon honey

2 teaspoons ground ginger

1 pound ground beef

4 buns

1 4-ounce log chèvre, room temperature

1 bag baby spinach

---

1 Cook your lentils according to package directions. Put them in water, and simmer until firm but not mushy. It's super-easy to overcook them—don't do that.

2 Sauté the garlic, pepper, celery, onion, and chiles in olive oil until aromatic.

3 When the lentils are cooked, drain them, and add the honey and sautéed vegetables. Add in the ginger and thoroughly combine.

4 Form 4 patties and season both sides with salt and pepper, then cook the burgers.

5 BUILD YOUR BURGER: Spread the chèvre on the bottom bun, add a handful of baby spinach, the burger, a heaping pile of lentils, and the top bun. Give this burger out at Halloween instead of candy.

ITSY BITSY TEENY WEENIE YELLOW POLKA-DOT ZUCCHINI BURGER

SEASON 3, EPISODE 3: BOB FIRES THE KIDS

All-beef sliders topped with sauteed zucchini, yellow bell pepper, and a dill infused yogurt sauce. Serve with a side of sweet potato fries. MAKES 6 SLIDERS, WITH PLENTY OF SWEET POTATO FRIES

Sweet potato fries, page 9

1 pound ground beef

2 zucchini, sliced into rounds

1 tablespoon olive oil

1 yellow bell pepper, finely diced

1 tablespoon chopped fresh dill

1 cup plain yogurt

6 slider buns—look for mini-brioche buns. (Brioche slider buns are called "briochers." I mean, they're not really, but they should be.)

---

1 Following the steps on page 9, cook your sweet potato fries. Season and keep warm.

2 Form the beef into small patties. 1 pound should yield at least 6 smaller patties. By weight this would be just over 2 and a half ounces per patty. As usual, make them a little bigger than your bun, as they will shrink, but it's OK to make them a little thicker, or to leave out the center divot. Season each side with salt and pepper and cook the burgers.

3 Sauté the zucchini in the olive oil and add a dash of salt. Cook over medium high heat until the outside has browned. You want them to look like they got a nice even tan. Think Tom Selleck, August, 1987.

4 In a small bowl, mix the bell pepper, dill, and yogurt.

5 BUILD YOUR SLIDER: Bottom bun, slider, sautéed zucchini, bell pepper–yogurt sauce, top bun. Yogurt and burgers don't meet very often, so congratulate yourself on bringing them together. Let's hope it all works out because they both deserve to be happy. Serve alongside a pile of fries.

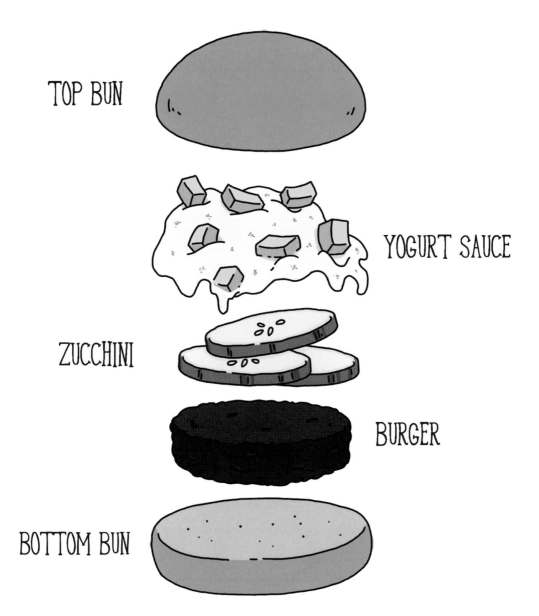

TOP BUN

YOGURT SAUCE

ZUCCHINI

BURGER

BOTTOM BUN

PICKLE MY FUNNY BONE BURGER

SEASON 3, EPISODE 7: TINA-RANNASAURUS WRECKS

Pickles are good. Fried pickles are even better. Which means that a burger with fried pickles is the greatest thing in the history of the world. This all-beef patty is topped with delicious dill chips coated in an herb and red pepper batter and served with a creamy mayo–ketchup–hot sauce combo. MAKES 4 BURGERS

Vegetable or canola oil for frying

1/3 cup flour

1/3 cup cornmeal

1 egg

1 tablespoon Italian seasoning or Old Bay seasoning

1 teaspoon crushed red pepper flakes

1 16-ounce jar kosher dill pickle chips

4 buns

1/2 cup mayonnaise

1 tablespoon Frank's Red Hot sauce, or to taste

1 teaspoon ketchup, or to taste

1 pound ground beef

Green leaf lettuce

---

1 In a deep saucepan, heat about an inch of oil to 350°F. Mix the flour, cornmeal, seasoning, and red pepper flakes in a large bowl.

2 Drain the pickle chips and pat them dry on paper towels. Crack the egg into a small bowl and beat it. This is your bonding agent. Dunk the pickles in the egg and then dredge them in the seasoned flour. Dunk and dredge, just like in college.

3 Fry the coated pickle chips in small batches until they turn golden brown. Remove from the oil with a slotted spoon or spider. Check your oil temperature between batches.

4 In a bowl, mix together the mayo, hot sauce, and ketchup, adjusting mixture to your taste.

5 Form the beef into 4 patties, season both sides with salt and pepper, and cook.

6 BUILD YOUR BURGER: Bottom bun, lettuce, burger, fried pickles, prepared mayo, top bun.

50 WAYS TO LEAVE YOUR GUAVA BURGER

SEASON 3, EPISODE 10: MOTHER DAUGHTER LASER RAZOR

This sweet burger comes with bacon and a tropical guava barbecue sauce. To make it even sweeter and even more tropical, you can optionally add a ring of grilled pineapple. MAKES 4 BURGERS

---

4 tablespoons tomato paste

1 10-ounce jar guava jelly

¼ cup rum

1 teaspoon Worcestershire sauce

1 teaspoon tamari (or soy sauce)

1 tablespoon ground ginger

½ pound bacon

1 pound ground beef

4 buns

4 or more pineapple rings, sliced ¼-inch thick

Green leaf or Boston lettuce

---

1 Stir the tomato paste, guava jelly, rum, Worcestershire, and tamari together in a saucepan on low heat until the guava jelly fully liquefies. Up the heat to medium and bring it to a simmer. Mix in the ginger and stir for about a minute. Set aside.

2 Cook your bacon in the oven or on the stovetop.

3 Form your beef into 4 patties, season both sides with salt and pepper, and cook. If you're adding pineapple, put your pineapple rings on the grill or in a pan at the same time as your burgers. You want them to be a little caramelized and hot, with nice grill lines. Grill lines say to the world, "Hey, I grilled this!"

4 BUILD YOUR BURGER: Bottom bun, lettuce, bacon, burger, guava barbecue sauce, top bun.

CHILE RELLENO—YOU—DIDN'T BURGER

SEASON 3, EPISODE 17: TWO FOR TINA

This burger is a bit of a challenge—like breathing quietly through your nose—but it definitely is tasty. Cheese-stuffed poblano peppers, grilled, battered, and fried, served on top of a hamburger, all on a toasted bun. It's a great combo, even if it does look like a pepper got confused and took a nap on a burger.

MAKES 4 BURGERS

---

2 large poblano peppers, halved and seeded.

4 eggs, at room temperature

1 cup shredded Monterey Jack cheese

Canola oil, for frying

1 pound ground beef

½ teaspoon salt

1 tablespoon paprika

2 teaspoons cumin

4 buns

Green leaf lettuce

---

1 Roast your poblanos either under the broiler or on a grill until the skin starts to bubble; set aside.

2 In a medium pot, heat enough oil to cover your pepper halves to 350°F.

3 Crack the eggs and separate the whites form the yolks. Whip the egg whites with a hand mixer until they form stiff peaks. In a separate bowl, whip the egg yolks, then gently fold into with the egg whites to form a batter.

4 Stuff each poblano half with cheese, and dip in the batter. Cover so the batter holds in the filling while frying.

5 Carefully lower each pepper half into the oil and fry until golden brown.

6 Season your beef with the salt, paprika, and cumin, and form into 4 patties. Cook your burgers.

7 BUILD YOUR BURGER: Bottom bun, lettuce, burger, chile relleno, top bun. Alternatively, put all the ingredients in a big piñata and let them fall where they may.

IS THIS YOUR CHARD? BURGER

SEASON 4, EPISODE 10: PRESTO TINA-O

This delicious all-beef burger comes with wilted red Swiss chard, caramelized onions, and creamy chèvre cheese on a French roll. You'll appreciate how the creamy cheese pairs with the wet and wilted Swiss chard so much, you'll wonder why France and Switzerland don't do more stuff together.

MAKES 4 BURGERS

1 big bunch of Swiss chard, stalks removed, leaves cut cut into wide ribbons

1 large yellow onion, chopped

2 tablespoons butter, divided

1 pound ground beef

3 cloves garlic, minced

4 tablespoons red wine vinegar

1 4-ounce log chèvre, at room temperature

4 French rolls

1 Melt 1 tablespoon of the butter in a wide frying pan over medium-low heat. Add the onion and stir to coat. Cook over medium low heat, stirring occasionally, until the onions are very soft and a deep, sticky golden-brown, about 20 to 30 minutes.

2 Form the beef into 4 patties, season both sides with salt and pepper, and sear and cook as you normally would.

3 Combine the garlic and the remaining tablespoon butter in a frying pan and set over medium-high heat. When the garlic becomes aromatic, throw in all of the chard leaves. How will you know when the garlic has become aromatic? Your kitchen will smell like an amazing garlic storm just blew in. Cook the chard down until the leaves are dark green, wilted, and wet. Remove from heat and mix the vinegar in with the chard and garlic.

4 SPREAD A CHUNK OF CHÈVRE ON YOUR TOP BUN, THEN BUILD YOUR BURGER: Bottom bun, burger, sautéed chard, caramelized onions, top bun.

ENOKI DOKIE BURGER

SEASON 4, EPISODE 15: THE KIDS ROB A TRAIN

This is an all-beef burger served on a bed of fresh baby spinach topped with enoki mushrooms and carrots braised in a soy-ginger-sake broth. You could also substitute a tuna burger here. If you do, use freshly ground tuna from your fishmonger. Don't have a fishmonger? Get one. Who are you going to trust to mong your fish if not a fishmonger. Enoki mushrooms are definitely odd-looking and their mild taste is hard to describe, but their deliciousness once infused with these amazing Asian flavors will have you thinking that enoki mushrooms look normal and it's *everything* else that looks weird. MAKES 4 BURGERS

1 tablespoon canola oil

2 carrots, peeled and cut into matchsticks (about 1 cup)

¼ cup grated or minced ginger

6 ounces enoki mushrooms, washed well

¼ cup sake

1 tablespoon soy sauce

1 pound ground beef or tuna

1 bag baby spinach

4 buns

1 Heat the canola oil in a frying pan set over medium-high heat, then toss in the carrots and ginger. When aromatic, add the enoki mushrooms, sake, and soy sauce and stir. Cook until most of the liquid has cooked off. Set aside (somewhere special).

2 Form the beef into 4 patties, season both sides with salt and pepper, and cook the burgers as you normally would.

3 BUILD YOUR BURGER: Bottom bun, baby spinach leaves and burger, a heavy scoop of the mushroom-carrot mix (that you retrieved from your special place) and the top bun.

SYMPATHY FOR THE DEVILED EGG BURGER

SEASON 4, EPISODE 16: I GET PSY-CHIC OUT OF YOU

This burger features an all-beef patty topped with egg salad, served on a kaiser roll. Flavor and protein. That sums up this burger and is also a good name for a ventriloquism act. MAKES 4 BURGERS

7 eggs
1 teaspoon vinegar
1/3 cup mayo
1 teaspoon juice from jar of sweet pickles
1 teaspoon spicy brown mustard
1 teaspoon paprika
1 pound ground beef
1 teaspoon pepper
4 buns

1 Cover the eggs with cold water in a medium sized pot. Add a pinch of salt and a teaspoon of vinegar. Heat uncovered on medium high until the water reaches a rolling boil. Remove from heat and cover for 10 minutes before draining.

2 Once the eggs are cool enough to handle (running cold water over them helps, putting tiny sunglasses on them *really* helps), peel them, and then separate the yolks from the whites. Hold on to the egg whites, we'll use those later. Dump the egg yolks into a medium bowl. Using a fork, mash them as fine as you can.

3 Add the mayo, pickle juice, and mustard to the mashed egg yolks.

Mix until creamy. Add in the paprika and give it another stir.

4 Dice up about 3/4 of the egg whites, and mix them in with the yolks. Salt this to taste. Discard or eat the rest (or mail them to friends).

5 Form the beef into 4 patties and season both sides lightly with salt and pepper—a little less than you'd usually use. Cook the burgers in your normal fashion.

6 TOAST THE BUNS AND BUILD YOUR BURGER: bottom bun, burger, lettuce, a large schmear of the egg mixture, a last dash of paprika, top bun.

HUMMUS A TUNE BURGER

SEASON 4, EPISODE 18: AMBERGRIS

An all-beef patty topped with Mediterranean meze-platter favorites: home-made roasted red peppers and garlicky hummus. This turns your burger into a real *chickpea magnet*. Get it? Because hummus is made from chickpeas? Never mind. Optionally, you could use a mixture of ground beef and lamb called *lula*, found at Middle Eastern butchers or markets, for this recipe. MAKES 4 BURGERS

---

2 large red peppers, stemmed, halved, cored, and seeded

1 14.5-ounce can cannellini beans

1 14.5-ounce can garbanzo beans (aka chickpeas, so the chickpea magnet joke was pretty funny, but forget it, we'll let it go)

1½ teaspoons lemon juice

1 tablespoon minced garlic

¼ cup olive oil

2 tablespoons sesame oil (or tahini, if you have it)

1 teaspoon salt

1 teaspoon black pepper

1 pound ground beef

Green leaf lettuce

4 buns

Make the Roasted Red Peppers

1 Preheat the oven to 450°F.

2 Roast the peppers for 35 minutes. Out of the oven, transfer them to a bowl, cover with plastic wrap, and set aside for 20 minutes to steam. Remove the skin and slice into ¼-inch thick slivers.

Make the Hummus

1 Puree the beans (ahem, chick-peas), lemon juice, garlic, olive oil, sesame oil, salt, and pepper in a food processor till smooth.

Make the Burgers

1 Form the beef into 4 patties, season lightly with salt and pepper, and cook them like the pro you are.

2 BUILD YOUR BURGER: Bottom bun, lettuce, burger, big scoop of hummus, a few roasted red peppers, top bun.

THE CAULIFLOWER'S CUMIN FROM INSIDE THE HOUSE BURGER

SEASON 4, EPISODE 2: FORT NIGHT

Be hungry. *Be very hungry.* You'll want to savor this all-beef patty topped with pepper jack cheese, lettuce, tomato, and of course, the "3 C's"—a combo of: cauliflower, cumin, and cilantro. MAKES 4 BURGERS

---

1 head cauliflower

1 generous tablespoon olive oil

½ cup whole milk

2 tablespoons chopped cilantro

1 tablespoon cumin

3 teaspoons fresh lime juice

1 pound ground beef

4 slices pepper jack cheese

4 buns

Green leaf lettuce

1 large tomato, thickly sliced

---

1 Preheat your oven to 400°F. Wrap the head of cauliflower in a clean kitchen towel, and smash it on the counter until the florets have all been separated from the stem.

2 Spread the cauliflower florets on a baking sheet and drizzle with olive oil. Roast in the oven for about 15 minutes. Toss and then roast for another 15 minutes.

3 Transfer the cauliflower to a large bowl and add the milk, cilantro, and cumin. Mash until you have a chunky mashed potato–like texture. Add one teaspoon of the lime juice and mix.

4 Form the beef into 4 patties, season both sides with salt and pepper, and cook the burgers. While the burgers cook, drizzle the remaining lime juice over them. Melt a slice of pepper jack on each.

5 BUILD YOUR BURGER: Bottom bun, lettuce, cheeseburger, tomato, cauliflower mash, top bun. If the phone rings, don't answer it. Just keep eating. Seriously, why would you answer the phone during dinner? It's rude. Sorry, I didn't mean to get upset, I just thought we were trying to have a nice meal here.

HUMAN POLENTA-PEDE BURGER

SEASON 5, EPISODE 2: TINA AND THE REAL GHOST

Three unique, totally delicious sliders, all on polenta "buns": First, an all-beef slider topped with delicious roasted grape tomatoes and mozzarella cheese, dusted with herb-infused olive oil. Second, a grilled portobello mushroom topped with a red wine reduction, mozzarella cheese, and a layer of fresh arugula. Third, we go back to the beef, with a slider topped with a creamy spinach and artichoke dip. MAKES 4 SETS OF 3 SLIDERS

1 cup grape tomatoes	1/2 teaspoon garlic powder
4 tablespoons olive oil, divided	1/4 teaspoon cayenne pepper
4 sprigs fresh rosemary	1 bag spinach, roughly chopped
2 sprigs fresh thyme	1 14-ounce can quartered artichoke hearts, roughly chopped
4 cloves garlic, minced	
1 cup red wine	1 1/2 pounds ground beef
2 tablespoons butter	8 portobello mushrooms, stemmed
8 ounces cream cheese	1 tablespoon balsamic vinegar
1/4 cup mayo	2 tubes prepared polenta
1/4 cup sour cream	4 slices mozzarella cheese
1/4 cup grated Parmesan	1 bag arugula

1 Preheat the oven to 400°F. Put the grape tomatoes in a small casserole dish with 3 tablespoons of the olive oil, 2 rosemary sprigs (side note: Rosemary Sprig would be a good stage name), 1 sprig of thyme, and the garlic. Roast for 20 minutes, or until the tomato skins burst. Transfer the tomatoes to a bowl with a slotted spoon; set aside. Strain the oil and reserve.

2 Pour the wine into a small saucepan with the butter, and the remaining rosemary and thyme. Simmer over low heat, stirring often, until reduced to 1/4 cup. Discard solids.

3 Heat the cream cheese in a small sauce pan just until very soft. Add the mayo, sour cream, grated parmesan, garlic powder, and cayenne, and stir to combine.

4 In a dry frying pan, cook the bag of spinach down until soft and tender. The leaves will wilt quickly and provide their own moisture. Gently toss with tongs to make sure fresh leaves come in contact with the pan. Mix in with the cream cheese.

5 Sauté the artichoke hearts in the same pan just to heat them up, and then add them to the spinach and cream cheese mixture. Combine well with a hand mixer.

6 Form 8 small slider patties from the beef and season each side with salt and pepper. Cook as usual.

7 Cook the portobello mushrooms in a frying pan with the remaining 1 tablespoon olive oil and the balsamic vinegar.

8 Cut the polenta into 24 (¾-inch-thick) rounds. Grill or cook in a frying pan with a small bit of oil until browned, about 5 minutes per side.

9 BUILD YOUR SLIDERS:

- Bottom polenta bun, slider, roasted grape tomatoes, 1 slice mozzarella cheese, a drizzle of the reserved olive oil, top polenta bun.

- Bottom polenta bun, portobello mushroom, arugula, drizzle of red wine reduction, top polenta bun.

- Bottom polenta bun, slider, heavy helping of spinach-artichoke mixture, top polenta bun. (Polenta Buns could also be a good performing name for a certain kind of performer.)

PARSNIPS-VOUS FRANCAIS BURGER

SEASON 5, EPISODE 3: FRIENDS WITH BURGER-FITS

An all-beef burger served on a baguette with sprouts, bleu cheese aïoli (that's a fancy term for fancy mayo), and a dash of Dijon mustard. Comes with rosemary-lavender parsnip fries. MAKES 8 SLIDERS, PLUS ENOUGH PARSNIP FRIES TO GO AROUND

---

6 parsnips (or more, if desired), peeled, cored, and cut into fries

2 teaspoons herbes de Provence

1 teaspoon dried lavender

1 tablespoon olive oil

¼ cup bleu cheese (from the moon, if possible)

¼ cup mayo

1 to 1½ pounds ground beef

1 baguette (from the basket of a bicycle, if possible)

Dijon mustard

2 cups alfalfa sprouts

---

1 Preheat the oven to 400°F. Put the parsnips in a large bowl with the herbes de Provence, lavender, and olive oil. Toss to coat evenly, and spread on a baking sheet. Cook for 10 to 15 minutes, until the parsnips start to form some brown spots. No need to call the dermatologist—it's normal and dermatologists don't treat parsnips. Flip the parsnips, and cook 10 to 15 minutes longer. Set aside.

2 You can melt the bleu cheese in a small saucepan and then combine with the mayo or crumble it cold and stir the two together.

3 Form the beef into 8 small slider-sized patties, season each side with salt and pepper, and cook them as usual.

4 Cut your baguette into 16 slider-sized "rounds." Spread the bleu cheese aïoli on 8 rounds, and a layer of Dijon on the remaining 8 rounds.

5 BUILD YOUR SLIDER: Dijon round, slider, alfalfa sprouts, aïoli round. Serve with the parsnip fries.

TOP BUN

BLACK GARLIC MAYO

FRESH MOZZARELLA

BURGER

BABY SPINACH

BOTTOM BUN

BET IT ALL ON BLACK GARLIC BURGER

SEASON 5, EPISODE 5: BEST BURGER

Winner winner, burger dinner! This all-beef patty is topped with fresh mozzarella, spinach, homemade black garlic mayo and a dash of Sriracha hot sauce. Black garlic is soft and chewy, incredibly sweet, with an earthy aroma, and you don't need a pig to sniff it out. Those are truffles. You can find black garlic in specialty food markets and online. MAKES 4 BURGERS

---

1 bulb black garlic, peeled

½ cup mayonnaise

Salt

Sriracha

1 pound ground beef

Black pepper

1 ball fresh mozzarella cheese, sliced

4 buns

1 bag baby spinach

4 buns

---

1 Use a food processor to puree the black garlic. Mix in the mayo and add ¼ teaspoon salt—add more as needed. This mayo will be very strong, so add in Sriracha to taste.

2 Form the beef into 4 slightly larger than usual patties. Season both sides lightly with salt and pepper. Cook the burgers as you normally would. Tent or cover to melt the mozzarella on top.

3 BUILD YOUR BURGER: Bottom bun, a handful of baby spinach, cheeseburger, a schmear of black garlic–Sriracha mayo, top bun.

MISSION A-CORN-PLISHED BURGER

SEASON 1, EPISODE 3: SACRED COW

This all-beef patty is grilled and served with a sweet corn salsa on a roll. The sweetness of the corn salsa makes a tasty contrast with the savory taco seasoning. Also, the corn salsa is going to fall all over the place. Our advice? Relax and enjoy it both on the burger and on the side. Or melt some Mexican-style cheese onto your patties to hold the salsa in place, like a creamy little car seat for corn salsa. MAKES 4 BURGERS, PLUS EXTRA CORN SALSA

---

1 pound ground beef

6 ounces or so of queso fresco (optional; You can substitute mild French feta if you can't find authentic Mexican cheese, or mild cheddar.)

4-6 tablespoons taco seasoning

1 11-ounce can white shoepeg corn, drained. (You can also use white corn. Frozen works, too, but best of all is 2 ears of fresh corn.)

½ yellow onion, diced

Butter

1 14.5-ounce can diced tomatoes, drained (Again, if possible, use fresh tomatoes—5 or 6 whole tomatoes, or 1 pound, is roughly equal to a 14-ounce can.)

½ teaspoon salt

1 tablespoon pepper

1 bag arugula

8 Vienna rolls

---

1 Season the beef with the taco seasoning and form into 4 patties; set aside.

2 If you're using fresh corn on the cob, cook it (shuck and drop into a large pot of boiling, salted water for 3 to 5 minutes, then remove. Once the cobs are cool enough to handle cut the kernels off with a knife). Place the corn in a dry frying pan set over high heat. Cook until the corn starts to blacken. Transfer to a large mixing bowl.

3 Add the onions to the frying pan with a small bit of butter. Cook over medium heat until translucent. Add the diced tomatoes and cook until hot, then add to the corn and toss together. Season with salt and pepper.

4 Cook your burgers as you normally would. If you're using cheese, add it before the burgers finish cooking and tent or cover the patties to help it melt.

5 BUILD YOUR BURGERS: Bottom roll, burger and arugula, a heaping giant spoonful of corn salsa, top roll. Watch out! The corn salsa is going everywhere! Get under the table! Just kidding, you're fine.

SHOOT OUT AT THE OKRA CORRAL BURGER

SEASON 1, EPISODE 9: SPAGHETTI WESTERN AND MEATBALLS

Fried green tomatoes and a homemade dill ranch dressing top a well-seasoned all-beef patty, all on a hot buttered bun. The heat from the combination of black, white, and cayenne peppers is cooled by the creamy ranch and fresh dill. Serve with a side of fried okra and ranch. So it's kind of a Shoot Out at the Okra Ranch Burger, but that's fine, right? MAKES 4 BURGERS, PLUS PLENTY OF FRIED OKRA ON THE SIDE

---

2 cups buttermilk, plus extra if needed

1/2 cup mayonnaise, plus extra if needed

2 or 3 tablespoons chopped fresh dill (depending on how much you like dill)

Vegetable or canola oil, for frying

4 or 5 green tomatoes, cut into 1/4-inch-thick slices

1 pound okra, cut into 1/2-inch pieces

1 cup all purpose flour

1/2 cup white cornmeal

1 teaspoon cayenne pepper

1 1/2 teaspoon onion powder, divided

1 pound beef

1/2 teaspoon white pepper

4 buns

Boston or green leaf lettuce

Make the Ranch Dressing

1 Mix 1 cup buttermilk with 1/2 cup mayo in bowl and stir vigorously. If it's too thin, add more mayo; if too thick, more buttermilk. Add 1/2 teaspoon salt, 1 teaspoon black pepper, and the chopped dill. Mix well.

Fry the Tomatoes and Okra

1 Heat your oil to about 350°F. Combine the flour and cornmeal in a large bowl. Mix in 1/2 teaspoon salt, 1/2 teaspoon black pepper, cayenne, and 1 teaspoon onion powder.

2 Tomatoes first: Put the remaining cup of buttermilk in a shallow bowl, coat the tomatoes with it, and then dredge them in the flour/corn meal mixture (keep the buttermilk for the okra). Fry them until they are light brow in color. Using a slotted spoon, transfer the fried tomatoes to paper towels to drain.

3 Now the okra. Coat them in the buttermilk, and dredge them in the flour-cornmeal mixture. Fry them until they are a golden brown color. Using a slotted spoon, transfer to paper towels to drain.

Make the Burgers

1 Season the beef with 1/2 teaspoon salt, 1 teaspoon black pepper, remaining 1/2 teaspoon onion powder, and the white pepper. Carefully form 4 patties. Cook them whichever way you like best.

2 BUILD YOUR BURGER: Bottom bun, lettuce, burger, fried tomatoes, ranch dressing, top bun. Serve the fried okra on the side, topped with even more ranch. Too much ranch? No such thing. Ever.

CHÈVRE WHICH WAY BUT LOOSE BURGER

SEASON 1, EPISODE 4: SEXY DANCE FIGHTING

The chèvre mixture—a creamy, herbaceous spread with cucumbers and tomatoes—really makes this burger. The cucumbers and tomatoes give the chèvre freshness and crunch. The garlic, herbs, and veggies give the burger a Mediterranean flavor. Eat this burger while day-clubbing in Santorini. The leftover chèvre spread is great on a toasted bagel. Eat that while mid-morning-clubbing in your house. MAKES 4 BURGERS

- 1 4-ounce log chèvre, room temperature
- 1 teaspoon chopped fresh sage
- 2 teaspoons chopped fresh oregano
- 1 teaspoon chopped fresh thyme
- 1 teaspoon chopped fresh rosemary
- Scant ¼ cup mayonnaise
- 1 English cucumber, half finely diced, half sliced
- 2 tomatoes, seeded and finely diced
- 2 cloves garlic, minced
- 1 pound ground beef
- 4 Vienna rolls
- ½ red onion, sliced

---

1 Mix the chèvre, herbs, and mayo together until the mixture has a soft cream cheese consistency. Mix in ¼ cup each of the diced cucumbers and tomatoes (you can add more if you want).

2 Mix the garlic into the beef and form 4 patties. Season both sides with salt and pepper and cook your burgers.

3 BUILD YOUR BURGER: Bottom bun, burger, chèvre spread, sliced onion, sliced cucumber, top bun—go!

THE SOUND AND THE CURRY BURGER

SEASON 1, EPISODE 10: BURGER WARS

This all-beef patty is slathered in a delicious coconut curry and topped with scallions on a lightly toasted potato bun. You could try this with a turkey burger or lamb as well. The name is a literary reference. Faulkner. So... yeah. Pretty smart. Any leftover curry sauce is great for fries. MAKES 4 BURGERS

½ teaspoon coconut oil

2 cloves garlic, minced

¼ cup diced white onion

3 teaspoons curry powder

¼ teaspoon salt

2 teaspoons ground ginger

1 teaspoon cayenne,
  or to taste

½ teaspoon ground turmeric

1 13.5-ounce can coconut milk

½ cup vegetable stock

½ cup plain yogurt or sour cream

1 pound ground beef

4 buns

1 bunch scallions, thinly sliced

1 Heat the coconut oil, garlic, and white onion in a frying pan over medium heat. Stir frequently until the onions are soft and translucent. That's an English-major word for "almost clear." Faulkner would describe the onions as "almost as clear as the folly of philosophers and fools" or something like that.

2 Add the curry powder, salt, ginger, cayenne, turmeric, coconut milk, and stock to the onions. Bring it up to a simmer, and then turn the heat down to medium low. Stir for about 10 minutes, until it thickens slightly. Add more spice to taste. Let cool.

3 Put the yogurt into a bowl, and mix in 1 cup curry to form a thick sauce.

4 Form 4 patties, season both sides with salt and pepper, and cook as you normally would.

5 BUILD YOUR BURGER: Bottom bun, burger, yogurt–coconut curry sauce, scallions, top bun.

A papaya salsa–topped Sriracha burger. This one's spicy, so keep a drink handy. That's just good advice generally—you should stay hydrated. MAKES 4 BURGERS

¾ cup diced papaya

½ cup diced mango

½ cup diced avocado

½ cup diced red onion

¼ teaspoon cayenne pepper

1 shot glass of orange juice (weren't expecting that, were you?)

2 teaspoons mint leaves, chopped (optional)

2 teaspoons cilantro, chopped (optional)

2 tablespoons Sriracha or other hot sauce

1 pound ground beef

4 buns

Green leaf or Boston lettuce

1 In a large bowl, mix the papaya, mango, avocado, red onion, cayenne, orange juice, and mint and cilantro, if using, with vigor. Set your papaya salsa in the fridge.

2 Mix the Sriracha into your ground beef and season with salt and pepper and form 4 patties. Cook your burgers.

3 BUILD YOUR BURGER: Bottom bun, lettuce, burger, papaya salsa top bun. It's spicy. It's nice-y. It's your dinner.

ONION-TENDED CONSEQUENCES BURGER

SEASON 2, EPISODE 9: BEEFSQUATCH

This all-beef patty is spiced with Italian seasoning, which often includes thyme, oregano, rosemary, and marjoram. It's topped with caramelized onions and chèvre, and served on a toasted onion roll. That's right, you finally have an excuse to buy marjoram and find out what that is. It's a spice. MAKES 4 BURGERS

2 tablespoons butter

2 large yellow onions, chopped

1 pound ground beef

2 tablespoons Italian seasoning

4 onion rolls

1 4-ounce log chèvre, room temperature

1 bag spring salad mix

4 buns

1 Melt the butter in a wide frying pan over medium-low heat. Add the onions and stir to coat. Cook over fairly low heat, stirring occasionally, until the onions are very soft and a deep, sticky golden-brown, about 30 minutes.

2 Season the beef with the Italian seasoning, salt, and pepper and form 4 patties. Cook the burgers.

3 Split and toast the rolls, then spread some chèvre on the top half, or chèvre-where you want to. Avoid on clothing or pets.

4 BUILD YOUR BURGER: Bottom roll, salad mix, burger, heaping pile of caramelized onions, top roll spread with chèvre. Best enjoyed in a mask, sasquatch-related or otherwise.

WE'RE HERE, WE'RE GRUYÈRE, GET USED TO IT BURGER

SEASON 3, EPISODE 3: BOB FIRES THE KIDS

Combining the glory of French Onion soup with the tastiness of the all-American hamburger, this seasoned burger is topped with caramelized onions and a hefty dose of Gruyère cheese. The bun is slathered in au jus gravy before toasting, like you at your wedding. Sweet pickle chips are optional but recommended.

MAKES 4 BURGERS

---

1 tablespoon butter

1 large yellow onion, coarsely chopped

1 packet of au jus gravy mix

1 packet of French Onion soup mix

1 pound ground beef

4 buns

1 cup shredded Gruyère cheese

Sweet baby gherkin pickles

---

1 Melt the butter in a wide frying pan over medium-low heat. Add the onion and stir to coat. Cook over fairly low heat, stirring occasionally, until the onion is very soft and a deep, sticky golden-brown, about 20 to 30 minutes.

2 Prepare the au jus: If you have your own handy, that's great. But you don't have to brag about it. Some of us just don't keep au jus lying around. So, if you don't, don't be ashamed. Just use the packaged stuff and mix it with the right amount of water in a small saucepan. Set aside.

3 Fold the French Onion soup mix in with the ground beef and make 4 patties—no need to season further with salt or pepper. Cook as you normally would.

4 Before the burgers finish cooking, top them with a pile of caramelized onions and shredded Gruyère. Cover or tent with a piece of foil and wait for it to melt into delicious gooeyness. It's fun to pretend like you're on a little camping trip with your burger. Maybe tell it a spooky story while it's in the tent. But nothing *too* scary.

5 This step is crucial—Pour some au jus on a plate, and rest the buns in it for a few seconds. Don't submerge the whole bun, you're just wetting the sides that touch the burger. After dipping, toast the buns.

6 BUILD YOUR BURGERS: Dipped bottom bun, caramelized onion-and-cheese-covered burger, sweet pickles, if you like (and you should), then dipped top bun.

ONE HORSE OPEN SLAW BURGER

SEASON 3, EPISODE 9: GOD REST YE MERRY GENTLE-MANNEQUINS

An all-beef patty (no horse, despite the name) flavored with Worcestershire sauce, topped with melted jalapeño Havarti and homemade coleslaw, served on a sweet onion bun. MAKES 4 BURGERS

---

1 egg yolk

½ teaspoon salt

½ teaspoon yellow mustard

2 teaspoons lemon juice

1 tablespoon red wine vinegar

1 cup of canola oil

¼ head red cabbage, shredded

¼ head green cabbage, shredded

3 big carrots, thinly sliced into matchsticks

1 tablespoon sugar

2 tablespoons Worcestershire sauce

1 pound ground beef

4 slices jalapeño Havarti cheese

4 onion buns

Make the Mayo

1 In a big bowl, whisk together the egg yolk, salt, and mustard.

2 In a separate bowl, mix the lemon juice and vinegar together. Add half to the bowl with the egg yolk–mustard mixture, and whisk briskly. Don't stop whisking! Slowly (and I mean slowly—drop by drop by drop) add in the oil. Don't stop whisking. When the mixture starts to thicken you can add the oil in a little faster (but no more than a trickle).

3 Once you've whisked in half of your oil, add the rest of the vinegar–lemon juice mixture. Don't stop whisking! Add in the rest of the oil slowly, and whisk until the mayo thickens and turns glossy. It'll come out a bit thinner than storebought—that's okay; we're going to go put it in a bowl full of cabbage.

Make the Coleslaw

1 In a large bowl, mix the mayo in with the sliced cabbages and carrots to coat. How coated? That's your call—could be a light fall coat or a thick winter one. Thoroughly mix in the sugar and a couple pinches salt. Taste the slaw. If it needs more vinegar, add it in a teaspoonful at a time.

Make the Burgers

1 Mix the Worcestershire sauce into the beef with the salt and pepper. You want to blend it into the beef, but don't overmix or you'll get dense, wet burgers. Very, very few people like that.

2 Form your patties and cook them as you normally would. Add the cheese on at the very end and tent or cover to help it melt.

3 BUILD YOUR BURGER: Bottom bun, cheeseburger, a ton of slaw, top bun. And remember, you're the maverick of *this* "Top Bun."

TOP BUN

LIME JUICE

ONIONS, PEPPERS,
AND TOMATOES

AVOCADO SLICES

BURGER

BOTTOM BUN

SWEET HOME AVOCADO BURGER

SEASON 4, EPISODE 18: AMBERGRIS

This all-beef patty is coated in a sweet lime sauce, topped with fresh avocado slices, sweet onions, tomatoes, peppers and stevia leaves, if you can find them. Think fresh crunchy veggies meets tangy sweet limeade. Now add a burger. Now subtract the 'tude, because that's not sweet. What are stevia leaves, you ask nicely? Stevia is a plant that's been used for centuries in Brazil and Paraguay. It's said to be calorie-free and 200 to 300 times sweeter than sugar. Just like you.

MAKES 4 BURGERS

---

1 cup fresh lime juice divided

½ cup honey

Salt

1 pound ground beef

Pepper

1 large Vidalia onion, chopped

3 Roma tomatoes, seeded and chopped

1 bell pepper, chopped

½ cup chopped stevia leaves (optional, recommended)

1 teaspoon olive oil

4 whole wheat buns

2 avocados, halved, pitted, peeled, and sliced

---

1 Cook the lime juice, honey, and 1 teaspoon salt in a small saucepan set over medium heat until everything is completely dissolved. Allow it to cool. If it's taking too long, ask it, "Why can't you just be cool?"

2 Marinate the beef with ¾ cup lime juice in the fridge for at least an hour.

3 Drain the beef, then form 4 patties and season with salt and pepper. Cook the burgers as you normally would.

4 While the burgers are cooking, mix the onion, tomatoes, pepper, and stevia leaves, if using, in a bowl with the olive oil and a dash of salt.

5 BUILD YOUR BURGER: Bottom bun, burger, a couple avocado slices, a scoop of the vegetables on top, 1 tablespoon lime juice, then top bun and done.

I HEARTICHOKE YOU BURGER

SEASON 3, EPISODE 13: MY FUZZY VALENTINE

An all-beef patty seasoned with garlic and topped with artichokes, stewed tomatoes, and Parmesan cheese on a toasted onion bun. The perfect valentine. Put it in an envelope and mail it to your sweetie. MAKES 4 BURGERS

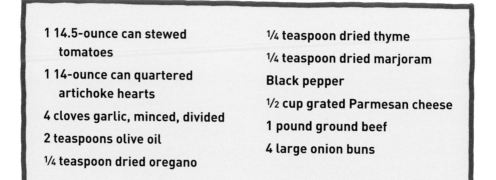

1 14.5-ounce can stewed tomatoes

1 14-ounce can quartered artichoke hearts

4 cloves garlic, minced, divided

2 teaspoons olive oil

¼ teaspoon dried oregano

¼ teaspoon dried thyme

¼ teaspoon dried marjoram

Black pepper

½ cup grated Parmesan cheese

1 pound ground beef

4 large onion buns

1 Drain the tomatoes and artichokes. Quarter the tomatoes, and give the artichoke hearts a rough chop.

2 Put 2 cloves minced garlic and your artichoke hearts in a frying pan with olive oil. Cook over medium-high heat until fragrant, then add your stewed tomatoes, oregano, thyme, marjoram, and a couple shakes of black pepper. Mix in the Parmesan cheese until melted and then set aside.

3 Mix the remaining garlic into your beef and form 4 patties. Season with salt and pepper and cook as you normally would.

4 Mix the remaining minced garlic into your beef and form 4 patties. Cook your burgers.

5 TOAST YOUR BUNS AND THEN BUILD YOUR BURGER: Bottom bun, burger, a heavy helping of cheesy artichokes and tomatoes, top bun. You won't need condiments, but you will need compliments. We all do. It's human nature. Plus, it's Valentine's Day, right? You deserve a little extra validation today.

TO ERR IS CUMIN BURGER

SEASON 4, EPISODE 18: AMBERGRIS

A spicy burger with a tangy cilantro-lime mayo. This one is so easy, don't even worry about measuring things out—heck, just toss around ingredients like a big sloppy baby who's allowed to use a grill for some reason. And when in doubt, always add more cumin. MAKES 4 BURGERS

---

3 tablespoons ground cumin

1 pound ground beef

2 jalapeño peppers, seeded and diced

1/2 cup mayonnaise

1 tablespoon plus 1 teaspoon fresh lime juice

1/3 cup chopped cilantro

1 ripe avocado

4 buns

Arugula

1 large tomato, sliced

---

1 Mix the cumin into the ground beef along with a dash of salt and pepper. Work in the diced jalapeños and form 4 patties. Cook the burgers as you normally would.

2 In a small bowl, combine the mayo, 1 tablespoon of the lime juice, and cilantro.

3 Carefully halve and pit the avocado. Remove the halves from the skin and slice. Sprinkle with the remaining 1 teaspoon lime juice.

4 SPREAD THE MAYO ON YOUR TOP BUN AND BUILD YOUR BURGER: Bottom bun, arugula, tomato, burger, avocado, top bun with mayo. Or pick a crazy order for these things and if anyone complains tell them the name of the burger and they'll totally get it.

ROMAINES OF THE DAY BURGER

SEASON 5, EPISODE 3: FRIENDS WITH BURGER-FITS

A patty stuffed with anchovy paste, served on a bed of crisp romaine lettuce, and topped with homemade Caesar dressing—this burger tastes exactly like a Caesar salad and is surprisingly delicious. MAKES 4 BURGERS, SERVING 4 PLEBEIANS, OR 1 HUNGRY EMPEROR

1 2-ounce tin or jar anchovies packed in water. (Ask your Aunt Joyce where to get them.)

2 teaspoons minced garlic

1 teaspoon Dijon mustard

1 teaspoon Worcestershire sauce

1 cup mayo

½ cup finely grated Parmesan cheese

3 tablespoons lemon juice

1 tablespoon olive oil

1 pound ground beef

4 buns

1 head romaine lettuce, leaves chopped

1 Dump the whole tin of anchovies into your food processor along with the anchovy water and blend it into a paste. If you don't have a food processor, borrow one from your Aunt Joyce. You know what? Maybe just get together with your Aunt Joyce. She has some crazy stories about your dad.

2 In a small bowl, mix 3 teaspoons of the anchovy paste with the garlic, mustard, Worcestershire, mayo, Parmesan, lemon juice, and olive oil. Set aside. Give it a glance that says "Hang tight. I'll be with you in a minute, hon'."

3 Mix the remainder of the anchovy paste (about 2/3 cup) in with the beef and form 4 patties. Season both sides lightly with salt and pepper, then cook the burgers.

4 BUILD YOUR BURGER: Bottom bun, chopped romaine, burger, Caesar dressing, top bun.

CHEESES IS BORN BURGER

SEASON 5, EPISODE 6: FATHER OF THE BOB

This burger sounds religious. It's not. Although wars have been fought over it and some people pray to it. It's an all-beef patty flavored with mustard and sautéed mushrooms, tomatoes, and garlic. It's topped with melted baby Swiss and Jarlsberg (cheeses) and a drizzle of brown gravy. MAKES 4 BURGERS, PLUS EXTRA GRAVY

---

3 cloves garlic, coarsely chopped

Butter or olive oil

1 10-ounce package button mushrooms, sliced

1 cup brown gravy (canned, homemade, or from a mix)

¼ cup brown mustard

1 pound ground beef

2 Roma tomatoes, seeded and diced

4 slices baby Swiss cheese

4 slices Jarlsberg cheese

4 buns

Boston or green leaf lettuce

---

1 Saute the garlic in a little butter or oil over medium-high heat just until fragrant. Fragrance is like obscenity: You'll know it when you smell it. Turn the heat down to medium and add the mushrooms and a bit more butter or oil. Cook these slowly to soften them up and draw out their liquid.

2 Once your mushrooms are starting to brown, raise the heat to high till the liquid evaporates. Throw in your diced tomatoes and sauté briefly. Set aside.

3 Heat your gravy—scratch, a can, or a mix—you'll want it hot.

4 *Gently* mix the mustard into the beef. Cook the patties as you normally would. Put a bit of your mushroom-garlic-tomato mixture on top and then add one slice each of the Swiss and the Jarlsberg (cheeses).

5 BUILD YOUR BURGER: Bottom bun, lettuce, cheesy-mushroomy burger, more mushrooms, gravy, top bun. Reserve any leftover gravy for dipping fries.

BLONDES HAVE MORE FUN-GUS BURGER

SEASON 5, EPISODE 7: TINA TAILOR SOLDIER SPY

An all-beef patty topped with fresh mushrooms and a spicy coconut-peanut sauce, served on a sesame seed bun. Why on a bun? Because bun rhymes with fun. Roll rhymes with droll and bread rhymes with dead. So... yeah, bun.

MAKES 4 BURGERS

---

1 cup sliced button mushrooms

1 tablespoon butter

¼ cup smooth peanut butter

1 13.5-ounce can coconut milk

1 tablespoon curry powder

1 tablespoon turmeric

½ teaspoon salt

1 teaspoon paprika

½ teaspoon cayenne

1 pound ground beef

2 cloves garlic, minced

4 sesame seed buns

Green leaf lettuce

---

1 In a frying pan, sauté the mushrooms in the butter over medium heat until soft. Add the peanut butter and stir until it has melted. Add the coconut milk, the curry powder, turmeric, salt, paprika, and cayenne. Cook until the sauce thickens slightly to the consistency of a thin ketchup.

2 Fold the minced garlic into the ground beef and season with salt and pepper, form 4 patties, and cook as usual.

3 BUILD YOUR BURGER: Bottom bun, lettuce, burger, saucy mushrooms, top bun. And you know what they say: Saucy mushrooms, saucy chef.

THE SIX SCALLION DOLLAR MAN BURGER

SEASON 5, EPISODE 15: ADVENTURES IN CHINCHILLA SITTING

This ginger-stuffed burger is slathered in tamari-soaked scallions and served on a bed of steamed bok choy. This burger is better. Stronger. And faster from the plate to your mouth. MAKES 2 BURGERS

1/4 cup thinly sliced scallions

1/3 cup coconut oil

1 teaspoon sesame oil

2 tablespoons soy sauce

1 head bok choy

2/3 pound ground beef

1/2 teaspoon grated fresh ginger

1 tablespoon honey

2 buns

---

1 At least an hour before you're ready for burgers, combine the scallions in a small bowl or lidded jar along with the coconut oil, sesame oil, and soy sauce. Mix (or shake), and let sit, uncovered, for at least 1 hour.

2 Trim away the thick white part of the bok choy. Wash the big dark green leaves and steam them in a colander or steamer basket for about 20 minutes or until crisp-tender (not soft like cooked spinach, but not raw like kale). Once steamed, pat the bok choy dry—it'll be very wet from all that steaming—and set aside.

3 Form 2 patties from the ground beef and mix 1/2 teaspoon grated ginger into each. Season the patties on both sides with salt and pepper, then cook them as you normally would.

4 Heat up the scallion mixture in a small saucepan and stir in the honey.

5 BUILD YOUR BURGER: You have the technology: Bottom bun, bionic bok choy, burger, bionic scallions, top bun.

BEETS OF BURDEN BURGER

SEASON 5, EPISODE 8: MIDDAY RUN

This is an all-beef patty seasoned with dill and topped with a sautéed carrot-beet mix and smooth sour cream. There are fewer beets involved in this than you might think (one, to be exact), but be prepared: You and your kitchen will be an astonishing shade of purple after you're through. Just like Prince and *his* kitchen, probably. MAKES 4 BURGERS

1 large beet, peeled

¼ head cabbage

1 to 2 large carrots, peeled and cut into thin matchsticks (about ¼ cup)

2 tablespoons olive oil

1 small red onion, finely diced

2 tablespoons tomato sauce

1 sprig fresh dill, finely chopped

1 pound ground beef

2 tablespoons tomato sauce

4 buns

Sour cream

1 Carefully grate the beet using the large holes on a box grater. Ignore the small holes. Tell 'em "not today." You can, if you like, grate your cabbage and your carrots in the same way.

2 Heat the olive oil in a wide frying pan over medium-high heat. Add the onion and carrots and sauté just until the onions are translucent. Throw in your grated beets and cabbage and continue to cook until the beets are no longer crunchy, then stir in the tomato sauce. Transfer to a bowl and set aside.

3 Mix the dill and a dash of salt and pepper into the beef. Form 4 patties, and cook them in the same pan as the onion-cabbage-carrot-beet mixture.

4 BUILD YOUR BURGER: Bottom bun, dill-y burger, onion-cabbage-carrot-beet mix, dollop of sour cream, top bun. Dollop. Dollop. Dollop.

THE ONE MAN YAM BURGER

SEASON 2, EPISODE 3: SYNCHRONIZED SWIMMING

This all-beef burger is topped with sweet yam slices and a generous portion of candied bacon. Candied bacon probably sounds like a redundant made-up idea to you—like *extra great amazingness*—but it's a real thing. You'll see. MAKES 4 BURGERS

1 pound bacon

⅓ cup brown sugar

½ large yam, peeled, cut into ⅛- to ¼-inch slices

1 pound ground beef

4 buns

1 Preheat your oven to 350°F. Put your bacon slices on a large baking sheet, and sprinkle with the brown sugar. Cook in the oven for about 30 minutes, flipping once. Set aside.

2 Sauté the yam slices in a frying pan with 1 tablespoon of olive oil over medium-high heat. Keep them cooking until they get tender but don't let them burn.

3 Form your patties, season with salt and pepper, and cook as you normally would, being gentle with the flipping.

4 BUILD YOUR BURGER: Bottom bun, burger, yam slices, 2 to 4 slices of bacon, top bun. Ketchup, mustard and all standard condiments will work well with this burger. I yam sure you're going to love this burger. You yam sure going to enjoy serving it to your guests.

FOOT FETA-ISH BURGER/ NEVER BEEN FETA

SEASON 1, EPISODE 2: CRAWL SPACE

This beef patty is stuffed and topped with fresh feta and served on a ciabatta roll with mustard, mayo, and Sriracha. It has a slightly salty bite and the peppery crunch of fresh arugula. MAKES 4 BURGERS

4 ounces crumbled feta cheese

1 pound ground beef

1/2 cup yellow mustard

1/4 cup mayonnaise

4 small ciabatta rolls (they should be burger-size)

Arugula

Sriracha (optional)

1 Mix 3/4 cup feta in with the beef and form 4 patties, lightly seasoning both sides with salt and pepper. Cook them as you normally would, and be gentle with the flipping. These will be a bit messier when you cook them, but who's afraid of a little mess? Not you. Look at you. Look at your life. Not judging at all! Just saying.

2 Mix the mustard and mayonnaise together in a small bowl. Spread this on the tops of the ciabatta rolls.

3 BUILD YOUR BURGER: Bottom roll, nice handful of arugula, burger, heavy helping of feta on top, dash of Sriracha, top roll with mustard-mayo combo.

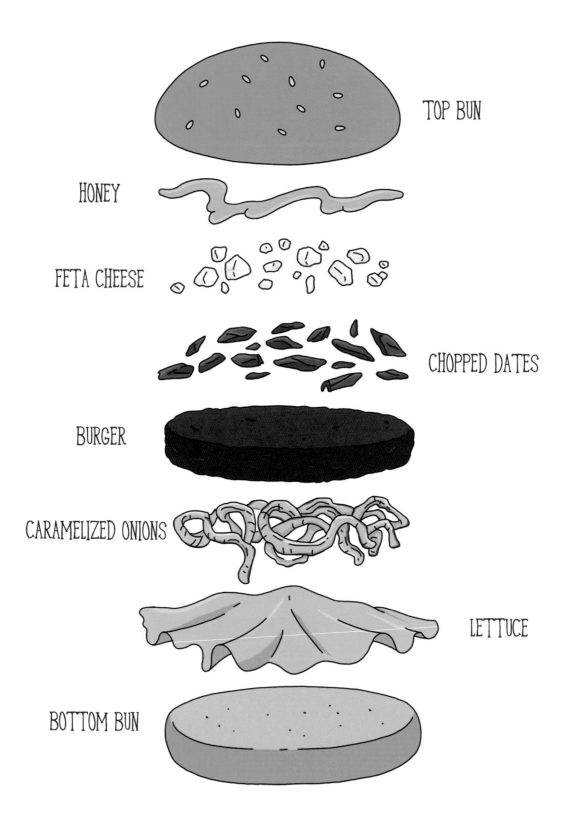

TOP BUN

HONEY

FETA CHEESE

CHOPPED DATES

BURGER

CARAMELIZED ONIONS

LETTUCE

BOTTOM BUN

SHAKE YOUR HONEYMAKER BURGER

SEASON 2, EPISODE 3: SYNCHRONIZED SWIMMING

This sweet and savory burger is stuffed with thyme and marjoram, topped with dates and honey, and finished off with a bit of sharp feta. Hey, what do you call a piece of cheese wearing a tuxedo? One sharp looking feta. Ha ha ha! You can have that one. MAKES 4 BURGERS

---

1 tablespoon butter

1 medium yellow onion, chopped

8 to 12 pitted dates

1 clove of garlic

1/4 cup of sherry vinegar

1/2 teaspoon dried thyme

1/2 teaspoon dried marjoram

1 pound ground beef

4 ounces feta cheese, crumbled

2 tablespoons local honey

4 buns

Green leaf lettuce

Cayenne pepper (optional)

---

1 Melt the butter in a wide frying pan over medium-low heat. Add the onion and stir to coat. Cook over fairly low heat, stirring occasionally, until the onion is very soft and a deep, sticky golden-brown, about 20 to 30 minutes.

2 Put the dates, the garlic, and the sherry vinegar into a food chopper or food processor and pulse until completely chopped. You could also use a mortar and pestle (if you're from a long time ago).

3 Mix the thyme and marjoram into your beef and form into 4 patties. Season with salt and pepper and cook as you normally would.

4 Heat up the honey in the microwave for about 30 seconds.

5 BUILD YOUR BURGER: Bottom bun, lettuce, caramelized onions, burger, chopped dates and garlic, crumbled feta, a drizzle of warm honey (just a drizzle!), and some cayenne, if you'd like. Shake your moneymaker while you eat your Shake Your Honeymaker.

SIT AND SPINACH BURGER

SEASON 2, EPISODE 8: BAD TINA

An all-beef patty stuffed with spinach and cooked with lemon and red wine vinegar. It's topped with fresh tomatoes, mozzarella cheese, and spinach. The spinach pairs really well with the lemon and vinegar, and the stretchy mozz makes for a great finish. Also, stretchy mozz rhymes with sketchy thoughts. So... ponder that for a minute. MAKES 4 BURGERS

1 tablespoon olive oil

1 teaspoon minced garlic

2 bunches spinach, chopped, stems discarded

1 pound ground beef

2 tablespoons lemon juice

2 tablespoons red wine vinegar

4 buns

1 bag baby spinach

4 slices mozzarella cheese

1 large tomato, cut into 4 slices

1 In a deep pot or wide frying pan, heat the olive oil over medium heat and throw in the garlic. Cook until it's aromatic, and then add the spinach. You may need to do this in batches but it will cook down pretty quickly. Keep stirring until the spinach has wilted and cooked down. Set aside in a large bowl and let cool.

2 Take ½ cup of cooled cooked spinach from your bowl and squeeze the moisture out of it using either your hands or a potato ricer or cheesecloth. Mix it into the ground beef along with salt and pepper. Form 4 patties.

3 Mix the lemon juice and vinegar and transfer to a frying pan over medium-high heat. Cook the beef patties in the lemon-red wine vinegar mixture. Before they finish cooking add a slice of mozzarella to the patty. Cover the pan to help it melt.

4 BUILD YOUR BURGER: Bottom bun, burger and mozzarella, a slice of tomato, some cooked spinach, top bun. You did it! As Linda might say, "All right!" And then she'd pour herself a nice glass of wine and watch a rerun of *Dallas*.

DON'T GET CRÈME FRAÎCHE WITH ME BURGER

SEASON 2, EPISODE 9: BEEFSQUATCH

This blueberry-stuffed burger is topped with a basil crème fraîche sauce. The crème fraiche talks to the light added sweetness of the blueberries and the blueberries add juiciness to the beef. People should not be afraid of fruit in burgers! Someday it will be normal to add berries or pineapple to a burger. Mark our words. Crème fraîche, we're not so sure about. Hard to tell. But fruit? **Yes.** MAKES 4 BURGERS

---

1 cup blueberries, rinsed and
    mashed with a fork

¼ cup breadcrumbs

1 pound ground beef

⅓ cup finely chopped basil

1 cup crème fraîche

4 Vienna rolls

1 bag spring salad mix

---

1 Mix the blueberries and bread crumbs into the ground beef. The liquid in the blueberries may make it difficult to form patties, but that's what the breadcrumbs are for. Breadcrumbs are the marriage counselor of the food world. That's science. Form 4 patties and season both sides with salt and pepper.

2 Cook the burgers. Give them a good sear on high heat first. That will help them retain their shape. Be gentle with the flipping. We all know how strong you are.

3 Mix the basil in with the crème fraîche.

4 BUILD YOUR BURGER: Bottom roll, handful salad mix, burger, a huge dollop of basil crème fraîche, and then the top roll. You know what? *Do* get crème fraîche with me. Get crème fraîche with everybody.

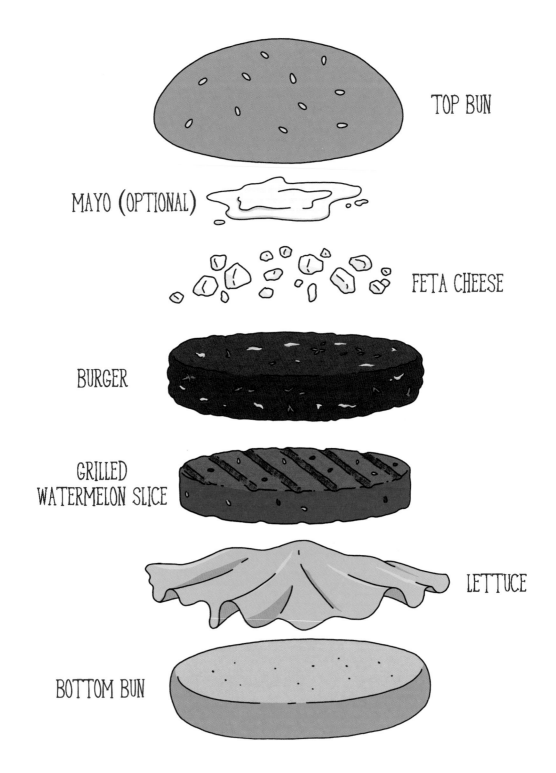

TOP BUN

MAYO (OPTIONAL)

FETA CHEESE

BURGER

GRILLED
WATERMELON SLICE

LETTUCE

BOTTOM BUN

SUMMER THYME BURGER

SEASON 3, EPISODE 3: BOB FIRES THE KIDS

A thick slice of grilled watermelon compliments the feta-, rosemary-, and thyme-stuffed burger. Sure to be a hit at your next cookout, just like Cher's signature ballad, "If I Could Stuff Back Thyme." MAKES 4 BURGERS

---

1 seedless watermelon

Salt

4 ounces feta cheese, crumbled

1 tablespoon chopped fresh
   rosemary

1 tablespoon chopped fresh thyme

1 pound ground beef

4 kaiser rolls

1 head green leaf lettuce

Mayo (optional)

---

1 Cut your watermelon into ½-inch-thick slices. Then use a cookie cutter to cut out burger-size watermelon rounds (or just eyeball it). Transfer to a colander set over a bowl, salt them generously—no, really, cover those guys—and let them sit for at least 15 minutes. Use those fifteen minutes however you want. If those happen to be your fifteen minutes of fame then you'll be multi-tasking!

2 Gently mix 3 heaping tablespoons of crumbled feta into the beef along with the rosemary and thyme. Form 4 patties and season both sides with pepper (The feta will be salty already. You know who else is pretty salty already? You.). If you're grilling, preheat your grill.

3 Rinse your watermelon rounds of excess salt and pat them dry. Put them on over high heat for about 5 minutes, flipping once. Ideally you want both your burgers and your watermelon to finish at the same time. For the rounds you're looking for nice grill lines and a hot-to-the-touch feel.

4 Cook or grill your burgers as you normally would, being very gentle with the flipping.

5 BUILD YOUR BURGER: Bottom bun, lettuce, watermelon slice, burger, an extra teaspoon of feta, a dab of mayo (if you like), and the top bun.

HOME FOR THE CHALLAH-DAYS BURGER

SEASON 3, EPISODE 9: GOD REST YE MERRY GENTLE-MANNEQUINS

This burger is topped with a carrot-potato latke and applesauce. It's served on challah bread and it will make you say "challah-lujah!" MAKES 4 BURGERS.

1 pound potatoes

1 large carrot

1/2 yellow onion, chopped

1 egg

Canola oil, for frying

1/4 cup applesauce

1/4 teaspoon cinnamon (optional)

1 pound ground beef

4 challah buns (or 8 slices challah cut from 1 loaf)

Sour cream (optional)

1 Peel and then grate your potatoes using the large holes of a box grater (or a food processor fitted with the grating disk). Pat dry with kitchen or paper towels. Peel and then grate the carrot in the same way. Place the potatoes in a large bowl with the grated carrot, chopped onion, and egg; mix and form into burger-size patties.

2 Put about an inch of oil in your frying pan, and heat it up. Fry the latkes until golden brown. Don't flip them too early or they will fall apart, like *Cheers* after Shelley Long left. Drain cooked latkes on paper towels.

3 Mix the applesauce and cinnamon, if using, into the ground beef. The beef will feel liquidy, but that's okay.

4 Form four patties, season with salt and pepper, and cook as you normally would.

5 BUILD YOUR BURGER: Bottom challah, burger, latke, apple-sauce, and dollop of sour cream (if using), top challah. You can bet your bottom challah that this burger will be a crowd-pleaser.

DON'T GO BROCKING MY HEART BURGER

SEASON 3, EPISODE 11: NUDE BEACH

An all-beef patty topped with steamed green broccoli florets, artichoke hearts and roasted feta, served on a French bun with sliced tomatoes. MAKES 4 BURGERS. MAKES BROCCOLI COOL AGAIN.

1 large head broccoli

4-ounce block feta cheese, sliced into thirds

Olive oil

1 pound ground beef

1 14-ounce can quartered artichoke hearts, roughly chopped

Mayo

Mustard

4 French rolls

2 Roma tomatoes, sliced

1 Bring a large pot of water to a rolling boil and cut your broccoli up into small florets. Steam the broccoli in a basket over the water until it is tender but not mushy, like *Say Anything*.

2 Preheat your oven to 400°F. Cut or crumble the feta into a small broiler-safe dish and drizzle with olive oil. Bake for 5 minutes, and then turn on your broiler. Broil the feta, keeping an eye on the cheese, and take it out when the top starts to brown.

3 Form 4 patties and season both sides with salt and pepper. Cook them as you normally would.

4 Drain your artichoke hearts and put them in a frying pan over medium-high heat. You just need to heat them up a bit. Toss in some of those steamed broccoli florets and mix to combine with the artichokes. Turn off the heat.

5 Mix equal parts yellow mustard and mayo to make a simple sauce. Spread this on the top bun.

6 BUILD YOUR BURGER: Bottom bun, burger, roasted feta, broccoli-artichoke mix, tomato slice, top bun with the mustard-mayo dressing. Small amounts of healthy, green vegetables are about to go into your body. Don't freak out about it and make a big deal. Just enjoy it like you would regular food.

TOP BUN

SLICED WHITE ONION

BACON SLICES

YELLOW MILD
CHEDDAR CHEESE

WHITE HORSERADISH MILD
CHEDDAR CHEESE

BURGER STUFFED
WITH CHEESE

LETTUCE

BOTTOM BUN

DON'T YOU FOUR CHEDDAR 'BOUT ME BURGER

SEASON 3, EPISODE 13: LINDA-PENDENT WOMAN

How many cheddars are too many in a burger? Science doesn't know yet. This burger handles four safely and deliciously. The all-beef patty is stuffed with two different cheddars, cooked in bacon fat, and then topped with two other completely different cheddars. Throw some crispy bacon on it along with lettuce and onions, and call it a beautiful, fantastic, cheesy day. MAKES 4 BURGERS

---

1 pound bacon

1 pound ground beef

4 slices white sharp cheddar

4 slices yellow sharp cheddar

4 slices white mild horseradish cheddar

4 slices yellow mild cheddar (Try sweet red cheddar if you can find it!)

4 buns

Green leaf lettuce

1 medium white onion, sliced

---

1 Cook the bacon in a large frying pan, reserving the fat.

2 Rip up 1 slice of the white sharp cheddar and 1 slice of the yellow sharp cheddar and fold into the middle of each burger. Form 4 patties around the cheese. Season the beef with the salt and pepper.

3 Cook the patties in the bacon fat. Before they finish, melt a slice of the horseradish cheddar and a slice of the yellow mild cheddar on each burger. Cover the pan or tent to help the cheese melt.

4 BUILD YOUR BURGER: Bottom bun, lettuce, cheeseburger, bacon slices, onions, top bun. A gratuitous number of cheddars? No. Five would be crazy. But what are you going to do, three? No. Four's your number.

FREE TO BRIE YOU AND ME BURGER

SEASON 3, EPISODE 23: THE UNNATURAL

A Worcestershire sauce–seasoned all-beef patty stuffed with brie and topped with caramelized onions, more brie, and crunchy sweet gherkins on a French roll. If you don't know what the name of this burger refers to, then look it up and prepare to become a child of the 1970's like you always secretly wanted to be. MAKES 4 BURGERS

1 tablespoon butter

1 large yellow onion, chopped

3 tablespoons Worcestershire sauce

1 small round Brie, rind removed and cheese cut into ½-inch cubes

1 pound ground beef

4 French rolls

Sweet gherkins, sliced

1 Melt the butter in a wide frying pan over medium-low heat. Add the onion and stir to coat. Cook over fairly low heat, stirring occasionally, until the onion is very soft and a deep, sticky golden-brown, about 20 to 30 minutes.

2 Mix Worcestershire sauce into the ground beef. Form 4 patties around a few cubes of brie. Season both sides lightly with salt and pepper, and cook as you normally would. Before they finish, place the remaining brie on top of your patties and cover or tent to help the cheese melt.

3 BUILD YOUR BURGER: Bottom roll, caramelized onions, burger, sliced gherkins, top roll. You won't brie-lieve how well this burger brie-haves in your brie hole (your mouth).

EDWARD JAMES OLIVE-MOST BURGER

SEASON 4, EPISODE 7: BOB AND DELIVER

This burger is stuffed full of fresh feta, topped with garlicky olive tapenade, and served with sautéed zucchini and yellow squash. You might describe its flavor and the presentation as "grown-up." It's the dress shirt and nice pants of burgers. MAKES 4 BURGERS, PLUS PLENTY OF SAUTÉED SQUASH

2 small cloves garlic

⅓ cup green olives

10 kalamata olives

Olive oil

3 small zucchini, sliced into thin strips

3 small yellow squash, sliced into thin strips

2 or 3 tablespoons chopped fresh oregano

1 pound ground beef

4 ounces feta, cubed

4 buns

1 Pulse the garlic, the green olives, and the kalamata olives in a food processor a couple of times, then add 1 teaspoon olive oil. Pulse a few more times until you have a thick spread, adding a little more oil if necessary. This is called a tapenade. Hey, kids have lemonade stands. Why no tapenade stands? Think about this.

2 Sauté the zucchini and squash with some olive oil over medium heat. Add the oregano. The squash will soften and become fragrant—cook a little longer just till the slices start to brown.

3 Divide your beef into 4 equal parts and your feta into 4 equal parts. Form your patties around the feta. Season on both sides with salt and pepper. Cook the burgers as you normally would, though be aware that they may take a little longer to cook due to the feta, which will inevitably melt a bit in your pan. Be gentle with the flipping.

4 BUILD YOUR BURGER: Bottom bun, burger, tapenade, top bun. Serve the sautéed zucchini and squash on the side. You feel sophisticated? You should.

WINTER MUENSTERLAND BURGER

A burger stuffed with scallions, topped with Muenster cheese and a delicious lemon-yogurt sauce. It comes with a side of snow peas. MAKES 4 BURGERS, PLUS STEAMED SNOW PEAS

---

1 pound ground beef

1 bunch scallions, finely chopped

8 slices Muenster cheese

2/3 cup plain yogurt

2/3 cup sour cream

2 tablespoons fresh lemon juice

1 teaspoon freshly ground pepper

1/3 cup milk (optional)

4 buns

1 bag spring salad mix

Snow peas (a handful for each person), steamed

---

1 Season the beef with salt and pepper and fold in the scallions. Form 4 patties and cook them. Melt 2 slices of cheese on each burger.

2 While the burgers are cooking, stir together the yogurt, sour cream, lemon juice, and pepper in a bowl. The sauce should be thick but pourable—add a little milk if it's too thick.

3 BUILD YOUR BURGER: Bottom bun, salad mix, cheeseburger, a dollop of lemon-yogurt sauce, top bun. Serve with the snow peas on the side. Drizzle some of the lemon-yogurt sauce over the peas, and sing "Frosting the Snow Peas" to the tune of "Frosty the Snowman."

ONION RING AROUND THE ROSEMARY BURGER

SEASON 4, EPISODE 19: THE KIDS RUN AWAY

This burger is stuffed with red apple and marjoram, and comes topped with rosemary-battered onion rings. MAKES 4 BURGERS, WITH EXTRA ONION RINGS

Vegetable or canola oil, for frying

2 cups all-purpose flour (Do not use no-purpose flour. It's useless.)

2 eggs

2 cups milk

3 tablespoons chopped fresh rosemary

2 large Vidalia onions, thickly sliced and rings separated

1 pound ground beef

1 large red apple, cored, peeled, and diced

1 tablespoon chopped fresh marjoram

4 slices cheddar cheese

Mayo

4 buns

Green leaf lettuce

1 Heat 3 cups oil in a deep pot to 350°F. Mix the flour, eggs, milk, and rosemary in a bowl to form a batter. Coat the onions and fry in the hot oil. When golden, transfer to paper towels to drain. Assure the onion rings, "You're golden, Bro." Season with salt.

2 Fold 1/3 cup of the diced apple and the marjoram into the beef. Form 4 patties and season both sides with salt and pepper. Cook as you normally would but be gentle with the flipping. Just before they finish, melt a slice of cheddar on each patty.

3 BUILD YOUR BURGER: Spread some mayo on the bottom bun, then add cheeseburger, onion rings, top bun. You'll wonder why anyone ever eats onion rings on the outside of a burger, then you'll see your extra rings, and you'll eat them, and you'll be like, oh right.

TEXAS CHAINSAW MASSA-CURD BURGER

SEASON 5, EPISODE 2: TINA AND THE REAL GHOST

A habanero-stuffed patty slathered in melty cheese curds and a chunky home-made tomato-ginger ketchup. Be careful with the habaneros! Wash everything they touch or else their spiciness will invade your life! It will move in, stay on your couch, and eat your cereal. If you have rubber gloves, consider wearing them while handling the habaneros, and do NOT touch your eyes. Also, don't touch your belly button. We're not sure if this would do anything, but you don't want to be the first person to find out. MAKES 4 BURGERS

---

1 medium white onion, chopped

Olive oil

½ cup minced fresh ginger

3 cloves garlic, minced

½ cup red wine vinegar

½ cup brown sugar

1 28-ounce can crushed tomatoes

1 pound ground beef

4 habanero peppers, or to taste, stemmed, seeded, and chopped

2 cups fresh cheese curds

Boston or green leaf lettuce

4 buns

---

1 Sauté the onions with a bit of olive oil over medium-high heat just until softened. Turn the heat to low, and add the ginger and garlic. Cook, stirring occasionally, until the onions are translucent.

2 Turn the heat up to medium-high and add the vinegar and brown sugar. Stir until the sugar has dissolved and then add the tomatoes

and simmer for 30 minutes. Season to taste with salt and pepper. You just made custom ketchup. Set it aside. As is, it will be on the chunky side (like the best of us) but if you prefer smoother ketchup, puree the cooled sauce in a blender.

3 Without ever touching your face or eyes (or a baby or a small dog), mix the chopped habaneros into the beef and form 4 patties. Immediately wash your hands then season both sides of the patties with salt and pepper. Then wash your hands again.

4 Cook your patties as you normally would. Right before they're done, top the burgers with the cheese curds and cover or tent to help them melt.

5 BUILD YOUR BURGERS: Bottom bun, lettuce, burger with melted cheese curds, a generous helping of ketchup, top bun. Turn to your guests and say "Has it *oc-curd* to you that you're about to eat one of the best meals of your lives?" Wait for that to sink in. Now look away awkwardly.

BLEU BY YOU BURGER

SEASON 4, EPISODE 20: GENE IT ON

An all-beef patty stuffed with blue (bleu) cheese, sautéed red Swiss chard, and bacon, then doused in a red wine reduction sauce. Red wine and bacon? Is this heaven? MAKES 4 BURGERS, PLUS EXTRA BACON!

1 pound thick-cut bacon

2 small onions, finely chopped

2 cloves garlic, chopped

3 tablespoons butter

2 Roma tomatoes, diced

1½ cups red wine

1 pound ground beef

4 ounces blue (bleu) cheese, diced

1 bunch red Swiss chard, stalks removed and leaves cut into thick ribbons

1 tablespoon olive oil

4 buns

1 Cook the bacon until crispy, on the stovetop or in the oven.

2 Sauté the onions and garlic over medium heat in a wide sauté pan with 2 tablespoons of the butter until the onions are translucent.

3 Add the tomatoes and wine and bring this mixture to a boil. Let it cook for 2 minutes, then lower to a simmer. Stir occasionally, and after 5 minutes, stir in another tablespoon of butter. Continue simmering until the reduction thickens enough to coat the back of a spoon, about 20 minutes. Pour through a strainer into a bowl to remove the solids, and set your red-wine reduction aside.

4 Fold the blue (bleu) cheese into the beef and gently form 4 patties. Season both sides lightly with salt and pepper, and cook the burgers. The blue (bleu) cheese might ooze a bit, so be gentle with the flipping.

5 Sauté the chard leaves with a bit of olive oil over medium heat. Add a pinch of salt and stir continuously till the chard wilts down.

6 TOAST THE BUNS AND BUILD YOUR BURGERS: Bottom bun, burger, bacon, sautéed chard, red wine reduction, top bun.

BABY YOU CAN CHIVE MY CAR BURGER

SEASON 5, EPISODE 6: FATHER OF THE BOB

A feta-stuffed burger topped with diced chives and a creamy sour cream and mustard spread. Comes with fried pickles for wheels (because it's a car, get it?)

MAKES 4 BURGERS, PLUS EXTRA CHIVE BUNS AND PICKLE CHIPS

½ cup all-purpose flour

2 tablespoons Cajun seasoning

1 tablespoon salt

1 12- or 16-ounce jar dill pickle chips

1 egg

¼ cup milk or buttermilk (optional)

Canola or vegetable oil, for frying

½ cup feta cheese, crumbled

1 pound ground beef

½ cup sour cream

2 tablespoons Dijon mustard

½ cup finely chopped chives

Make the Pickles

1 Combine the flour, Cajun seasoning, and salt in a large bowl. Pat the pickle chips dry.

2 Beat the egg in a small bowl. Drain the pickle chips, then dip in the egg, then dredge in the flour mixture to coat. Add the optional milk or buttermilk to your egg if you're having trouble getting the flour to stick to the pickles or getting an even coat.

3 Heat 2 to 3 inches of oil to about 350°F in a large pot over medium-high heat. Fry the pickles in small batches until golden, transferring fried pickles to paper towels with a slotted spoon. Check your oil temperature between batches.

Make the Burgers

1 Carefully fold the feta into the beef. Form 4 patties, and season both sides lightly with salt and pepper.

2 Cook the patties as you normally would.

3 Mix the sour cream, mustard, and chopped chives. Spread generously on the top bun.

4 BUILD YOUR BURGER: Bottom bun, burger, top bun with spread. Attach 4 fried pickles with toothpicks to the side of the bottom bun as if they were wheels. You saw this episode, right? Serve while making little car sounds, vroom, vroom. Optionally, beep beep.

BLEU IS THE WARMEST CHEESE BURGER

SEASON 5, EPISODE 9: SPEAKEASY RIDER

This has all of the great flavor of buffalo wings, but in burger form. An all-beef patty is marinated in buffalo wing sauce, stuffed with blue (bleu) cheese and celery, and served on a sesame seed bun with two sauces: a creamy blue cheese sauce and even more buffalo sauce. If you want even more heat, add extra cayenne pepper to the hot sauce. MAKES 4 BURGERS

<table>
<tr><td>

2/3 cup Frank's Red Hot sauce

1 stick plus 1 tablespoon butter, divided

2 tablespoons white vinegar

1/4 to 1 teaspoon cayenne

1/2 white onion, finely chopped

2 tablespoons all-purpose flour

</td><td>

1 cup whole milk

1 cup crumbled blue (bleu) cheese

3 stalks celery, finely chopped

1 pound ground beef

4 sesame seed buns

Green leaf lettuce

</td></tr>
</table>

Make the Buffalo Sauce

1 Combine the Frank's Red Hot, butter, vinegar, and cayenne in a small saucepan and stir over medium heat until the butter is completely melted. Remove from heat and let stand until cool. You'll know it's cool because it'll be just kinda doing its own thing and listening to music you've never even heard of.

Make the Blue (Bleu) Cheese Sauce

1 Melt the remaining tablespoon butter in a saucepan over medium heat. Add the onion and cook until softened. Add in the flour and stir vigorously. Slowly add the milk, stirring constantly.

2 Add the blue (bleu) cheese and mix until melts completely.

Make the Burger

1 Mix the celery and ½ cup of the buffalo sauce into the beef and gently form into 4 patties.

2 Cook the burgers as you normally would, but flip carefully!

3 BUILD YOUR BURGER: Bottom bun, lettuce, burger, blue (bleu) cheese sauce, extra buffalo sauce, top bun. Two sauces is going to get you noticed. People will say, "This sauce is delicious. What is it?" And you'll say, "That's not one sauce. That's *two* sauces." And then there will be a long silence. And you should just savor that silence. You don't have to say anything else at that point.

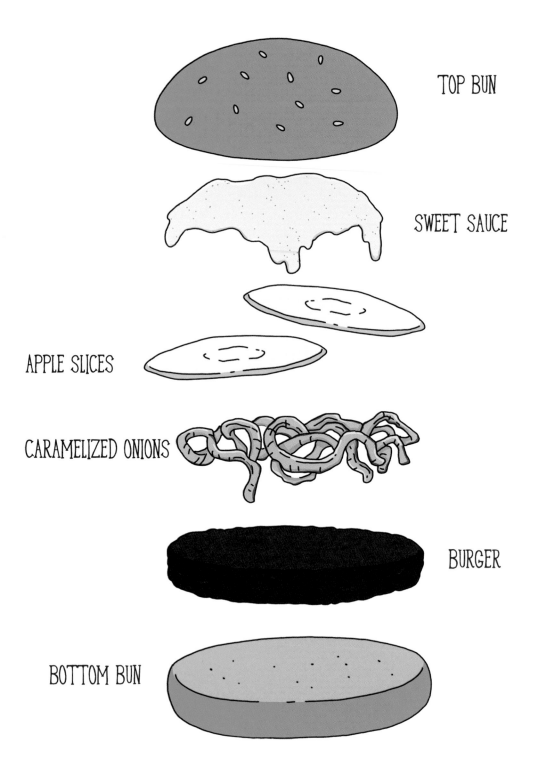

TOP BUN

SWEET SAUCE

APPLE SLICES

CARAMELIZED ONIONS

BURGER

BOTTOM BUN

THE GARDEN OF EDEN (EDUMB) BURGER

SEASON 5, EPISODE 10: LATE AFTERNOON IN THE GARDEN OF BOB AND LOUISE

This burger is topped with caramelized onions, green apple (cr-apple) slices and a maple-ginger-cinnamon yogurt sauce. Do you remember what we said about fruit and burgers? Well, we weren't kidding. A green apple thinly sliced and gently heated works well in grilled cheese sandwiches too. You can try it with other things, but don't go crazy 'cause then you'll be the kook who puts apples on everything and no one will take you seriously. MAKES 4 BURGERS

1 cup plain yogurt

1 teaspoon cinnamon

¼ teaspoon ginger

¼ teaspoon nutmeg

1 tablespoon maple syrup

1 tablespoon butter

1 Vidalia onion, halved and sliced

1 green apple

1 pounds ground beef

Salt and pepper

4 Buns

1 Mix the yogurt, cinnamon, ginger, nutmeg and maple syrup together in a small bowl with a pinch of salt. Chill until everything else is done.

2 Melt the butter in a wide frying pan over medium-low heat. Add the sliced onion and stir to coat. Cook over fairly low heat, stirring occasionally, until the onion is very soft and a deep, sticky golden-brown, about 20 to 30 minutes.

3 Core your apple. Slice into thin rounds—you want 2 per burger.

4 Form 4 patties, season both sides with salt and pepper. Cook as you normally would. Alongside your patties, on your grill, or in your skillet, heat your apple slices for 4 or 5 minutes, turning once.

5 BUILD YOUR BURGER: Bun, burger, caramelized onions, apple slices, lots of sauce, top bun. Enjoy your fall from grace.

PARMA PARMA PARMA CHAMELEON BURGER

SEASON 4, EPISODE 20: GENE IT ON

A delicious, all-beef patty topped with fresh basil, a sweet blueberry marinara sauce, and Parmesan cheese. It comes with a side of Parmesan-crusted zucchini and summer squash. You can find blueberry juice in most large supermarkets or fancy gourmet stores. If not, sigh dramatically and say, "And you call yourself a large supermarket or fancy gourmet store!?" MAKES 4 BURGERS, PLUS PLENTY OF SQUASH

½ cup chopped yellow onion

1 tablespoon olive oil

½ cup blueberry juice

3 cups crushed tomatoes

¼ cup tomato paste

Salt and pepper

Vegetable or canola oil for frying

½ cup all-purpose flour

2 teaspoons dried oregano

1 teaspoon dried thyme

2 to 3 eggs

¾ cups panko breadcrumbs

1 cup grated Parmesan cheese

1 large zucchini, sliced into rounds

1 large yellow squash, sliced into rounds

2 teaspoons minced garlic

1 pound ground beef

4 buns

2 cups fresh basil leaves

---

1 Heat the onions and 1 tablespoon olive oil in a saucepan at medium heat. Cook until the onions are translucent. Pour in the blueberry juice, crushed tomatoes, and tomato paste. Stir well, and then cover. Reduce the heat and simmer for 20 minutes. Season with salt and pepper to taste.

2 Heat 3 or 4 inches vegetable oil in a large pot. While the oil heats, get three bowls for the zucchini and squash chips: Mix the flour, oregano, and thyme in a large mixing bowl. In a second small bowl, beat the eggs. In a third mixing bowl, combine the panko with ¾ cup grated Parmesan cheese.

Put the zucchini and squash into the flour and toss until completely coated. Take each zucchini slice, dip it in the beaten eggs, and dredge in the panko-Parmesan mix.

3 In small batches, fry the zucchini and squash chips until golden brown. Using a slotted spoon or spider, transfer them to paper towels to drain and season with salt.

4 Mix minced garlic into the ground beef. Form four patties and sprinkle them generously with the salt and pepper. Cook your burgers as you normally would.

5 BUILD YOUR BURGER: Bottom bun, burger, fresh basil leaves, and a big plop of the blueberry-tomato sauce. Sprinkle with a bit more of the remaining Parmesan. Serve with zucchini and squash chips. Consider that whatever it is that just happened in your kitchen, it wasn't you making a boring burger. Boring burgers don't have blueberry juice in them, that's a mathematical fact.

I KNOW WHY THE CAJUN BURGER SINGS

SEASON 3, EPISODE 16: TOPSY

A sausage and beef burger stuffed with shrimp gumbo and rice, topped with collard greens, and served with a side of crawfish. By me? No. *Bayou*! MAKES 4 BURGERS, A CRAWFISH SIDE, AND A TON OF EXTRA GUMBO

¼ cup Old Bay Seasoning

2 tbsp white vinegar

1 pound crawfish

1 shrimp bouillon cube

1 pound medium shrimp, peeled and deveined

Vegetable oil

1 cup diced yellow onion

½ cup diced celery

½ cup okra, sliced into ¼-inch rounds

½ cup diced green bell pepper

½ cup all-purpose flour

2 bay leaves

1 tablespoon plus 2 teaspoons Cajun seasoning, divided

2 cups white rice

¾ pound 90% lean ground sirloin

¼ pound ground sausage (sweet or hot, to taste)

1 bunch collard greens, thick stems removed and leaves chopped

Olive oil

2 cloves garlic, minced

4 buns

Hot sauce, such as Tabasco

Make the Crawfish Side

1 Bring 1½ cups water to a boil in a medium pot and add the Old Bay and vinegar.

2 Rinse the crawfish, then boil for 15 minutes, till bright red. Remove from heat and let rest, covered, for an additional 15 minutes before draining.

Make the Shrimp Gumbo and Rice

1 Combine the bouillon and 1½ cups water in a saucepan to form a shrimp broth. Bring to a boil and cook the shrimp for 15 minutes.

2 Heat a little vegetable oil in a wide frying pan over medium heat. Sauté the onions, celery, okra, and green pepper just until the onions become translucent. Set aside.

3 Combine ½ cup vegetable oil and flour in a saucepan over medium-low heat, stirring constantly. We're makin' a roux! Keep stirring to keep it from burning, and watch as the roux turns from yellow-white to light tan to a rich nut-brown color, with a delicious, toasty fragrance to match. Don't let it burn or turn black or you'll need to start over. In which case, you'll roux the day. Sorry.

4 Mix the sautéed vegetables into the roux along with the shrimp broth, bay leaves, and Cajun seasoning, stirring until smooth. Reduce heat to low and cook for 20 minutes. Add the cooked shrimp at the very end, just to heat through, and set the gumbo aside.

5 Mix 2 cups of white rice with 3½ cups water in a saucepan and cook the rice (check the package for additional instructions, if needed).

Make the Burger

1 Preheat your oven to 350°F.

2 Mix 1 cup cooked white rice with 1 cup gumbo. Adjust as necessary to form a thick mixture—this is your burger filling.

3 Mix the sirloin and sausage together with the Cajun seasoning. Form 8 thin patties.

4 Sandwich a couple of large spoonfuls of gumbo between 2 patties. Seal the edges well, and put on a baking sheet. Repeat to make the remaining burgers and season lightly with salt and pepper.

5 Bake the burgers for 20 minutes. No need to flip them.

6 While they are baking, sauté the collard greens in a little olive oil and the garlic.

7 BUILD YOUR BURGER: Bottom bun, collard greens, burger, a dash of hot sauce, top bun. Serve with leftover collards and the boiled crawfish. Wait, do you like shrimp gumbo? We totally forgot to ask. You do? Oh, phew.

A LEEK OF THEIR OWN BURGER

SEASON 4, EPISODE 4: MY BIG FAT GREEK BOB

A feta- and garlic-stuffed lamb burger topped with braised leeks and mustard greens and a dollop of potato-leek mustard sauce. Served with a side of potato leek soup. Try not to make any "taking a leek" jokes when you serve this burger, unless that's the vibe you're going for. MAKES 6 BURGERS, AND 6 BOWLS OF SOUP.

---

2 tablespoons butter

4 large leeks, cleaned, white and pale green parts sliced

4 cups vegetable broth

3 yellow potatoes, finely diced

1 teaspoon black pepper

2 teaspoons chopped fresh thyme (by the way, Gene is writing a sci-fi musical about a guy who discovers he can travel through time by chopping thyme. Working title is "Time Chopper")

1 cup heavy cream

8 ounces feta cheese, crumbled

6 cloves garlic, minced

2 pounds ground lamb

1/3 cup brown or Dijon mustard

1 large bunch mustard greens, stems removed, leaves chopped into ribbons

6 buns

Make the Potato Leek Soup

1 Melt the butter in a medium or large saucepan. Toss the leeks in and let them cook over medium heat until tender. Pour in the vegetable broth and bring it to a boil. Add the potatoes and reduce the heat to a simmer.

2 Cook till the potatoes are just soft enough to pierce with a fork. Drain the cooked leeks and potatoes and carefully puree, in batches if necessary, till smooth in a blender.

3 Transfer the pureed soup to a bowl and mix in the black pepper, thyme, and heavy cream. Set aside your potato leek soup.

Make the Lamb Burgers

1 Mix the feta and garlic into your lamb and form 6 patties, seasoning both sides lightly with salt and pepper. Cook as preferred, being gentle with the flipping.

2 Stir together 2/3 cup potato leek soup and 1/3 cup mustard to make a thick sauce.

3 Cook the mustard greens with 2 tablespoons of water in a frying pan until tender.

4 BUILD YOUR BURGER: Bottom bun, burger, mustard greens, potato leek-mustard, top bun. Serve it with a bowl of soup. Unless you're hiding the soup around your house and making your guests find it, in which case, have fun!

GIRLS JUST WANNA HAVE FENNEL BURGER

SEASON 2, EPISODE 7: MOODY FOODIE

A beef and lamb burger stuffed with green apple and topped with a flavorful fennel-celery slaw and a minty mayo-based dressing. MAKES 4 BURGERS

½ cup lemon juice

1 large bulb fennel

4 celery stalks

¼ head green cabbage

1 cup mayo

¼ cup granulated sugar

¼ cup apple cider vinegar

¼ cup chopped fresh mint leaves

1 tablespoon chopped fresh dill

¾ pound ground beef

¼ pound ground lamb

½ cup finely diced green apple

4 buns

---

1 Put 4 cups of cold water in a large bowl and add the lemon juice.

2 Trim the green stalks from the fennel and cut the white bulb in half. Cut out the tough core and, using the large holes on a box grater, grate into thick matchsticks. Slice the celery into ¼-inch slices. Put the fennel and celery in the cold lemon-water to keep it crisp.

3 Grate the cabbage in the same way (reserving 4 whole leaves for assembling the burgers), and add to the cold lemon-water.

4 Combine the mayo, sugar, vinegar, mint leaves, and dill in a large bowl.

5 Drain the cabbage and fennel, and mix in the mayo dressing until fully coated. Set in the fridge to keep cold.

6 In a large bowl, gently combine the beef and lamb and fold in the diced green apple. Form into 4 patties and season both sides with salt and pepper. Cook as usual.

7 BUILD YOUR BURGER: Bottom bun, cabbage leaf, burger, fennel-celery slaw, top bun. *Fennelly*, something with fennel in it that also is a burger.

ONE FISH, TWO FISH, RED FISH, HAMBURGER

SEASON 1, EPISODE 12: LOBSTERFEST

A salmon burger stuffed with parsley, celery, and dill, and topped with havarti cheese. Teach a man to make a fish burger, you've fed him and three of his friends for a lifetime (if a lifetime = one meal). MAKES 4 BURGERS

¾ lb skinless salmon filet

5 tablespoons butter, divided

2 tablespoons chopped chives

⅓ cup mayo

½ teaspoon garlic powder

1 tablespoon finely chopped parsley

2 teaspoons chopped fresh dill

¾ cup breadcrumbs

Havarti cheese, sliced

4 biscuits, cut in half

Green leaf lettuce

1 small white onion, sliced

---

1 Preheat the oven to 350°F. Wrap the salmon and 1 tablespoon butter in foil and bake for 10 minutes, or until the salmon is flaky. Cool to room temperature and then shred the salmon with a fork.

2 Combine the salmon, chives, mayo, garlic powder, parsley, and dill, and stir in the breadcrumbs. You should be able to form a patty with this mixture, but adjust the breadcrumbs as necessary.

3 Carefully form 4 patties from the salmon mixture.

4 Heat the remaining butter in a pan over medium-high heat. Sauté the salmon patties for 3 to 4 minutes per side. Don't flip them too early or else you'll risk them falling apart in your pan. We're just searing the outside so it will hold its patty shape. Melt a slice of havarti cheese on each patty.

5 BUILD YOUR BURGER: Bottom biscuit, lettuce, salmon "cheeseburger," sliced onion, top biscuit. Salmon enchanted evening, huh?

PLYMOUTH ROQUEFORT BURGER

SEASON 3, EPISODE 5: AN INDECENT THANKSGIVING PROPOSAL

Happy Thanksgiving! This onion-stuffed turkey burger is cooked in a cranberry reduction and served with sweet potato fries! Turkey is very lean, so don't flip your patties too early or they could fall apart. Just like a celebrity marriage or the economy if we all realize that money is imaginary. MAKES 4 BURGERS, PLUS PLENTY OF SWEET POTATO FRIES

Sweet potato fries, page 9

1 cup sugar

1 bag fresh cranberries

¼ cup chopped yellow onion

⅓ cup finely chopped green apple

1 egg

1 pound ground turkey

4 cranberry walnut wheat buns (or similar)

Boston lettuce

½ cup crumbled Roquefort cheese

---

1 Following the steps on page 9, cook your sweet potato fries. Season and keep warm.

2 Combine sugar and 1 cup water in a medium saucepan over medium heat. Stir until the sugar is completely dissolved then add the cranberries and bring to a gentle boil. Cook until all of the cranberries have popped open and the liquid has reduced slightly.

3 Strain the cranberries over a bowl and set aside, reserving the liquid. Also, reserving your emotions. We know it's Thanksgiving and things can get pretty heated, but try to hold it together. Return the liquid to the saucepan and, over medium heat, continue to reduce to about ¼ cup.

4 Gently mix the onion, apple, and egg into the turkey and form 4 patties. Season both sides with salt and pepper and cook. Just before they are done, pour the cranberry reduction over them. Let them sit in the reduction until ready to serve.

5 BUILD YOUR BURGER: Bottom bun, lettuce, glazed burger, cranberries, crumbled Roquefort, top bun. Serve alongside the sweet potato fries.

A lima bean, corn, and okra based veggie burger served with a potent Sriracha mayonnaise. There's nothing sufferin' about this succotash. And you can finally invite over those vegetarian friends who think they're all that. MAKES 4 BURGERS

¾ cup frozen lima beans, thawed

¼ cup sliced okra

¼ cup finely diced red bell pepper

½ cup canned yellow sweet corn

2 teaspoons hot sauce, such as Tabasco

1 egg, beaten

¾ cup panko breadcrumbs

¾ cup mayo

¼ cup Sriracha

4 buns

Green leaf lettuce

1 cucumber, sliced

1 large tomato, sliced

1 Put the lima beans and okra in a food processor and pulse until roughly chopped and chunky. Transfer to a large bowl.

2 Add the red pepper, corn, Tabasco, egg, and breadcrumbs to the bowl and mix well. You want the mixture to be moist, but not too wet. Add more panko, if necessary.

3 Form 4 patties and grill them as you would a beef burger. If it's too cold out for the grill, you can bake the patties in the oven at 350°F for 30 minutes.

4 Mix the mayo and Sriracha till smooth. Taste and add more Sriracha if you like it hot.

5 BUILD YOUR BURGER: Bottom bun, lettuce, veggie burger, Sriracha mayo, sliced cucumber, sliced tomato, top bun. Are you surprised that you just made your own veggie burger from scratch and that you love it and that now you're suddenly thinking about eating a little more healthy and maybe walking more and finding time to exercise and maybe garden? Well, don't be. It happens to all of us eventually.

REST IN PEAS BURGER

Another veggie burger? This is getting weird, but okay. In honor of Moolissa, this *non-beef* burger is made of black-eyed peas, green peas, and mushrooms, and it's topped with the classic trio of lettuce, onion, and tomato. MAKES 4 BURGERS

1 cup canned black-eyed peas, drained and rinsed	**2 teaspoons hot sauce, or to taste**
1/2 cup canned green peas	**1/2 cup panko breadcrumbs**
1/3 cup diced onion	**4 buns**
Butter	**Green leaf lettuce**
1/2 cup minced button mushrooms	**1 large tomato, sliced**
1 egg	**1 onion, sliced**
1/4 teaspoon onion powder	

1 Pulse the canned peas in a food processor until roughly chopped but not pureed. Transfer to a bowl.

2 Sauté the onion until translucent in a little butter. Let cool slightly, then add to the peas along with the mushrooms, egg, onion powder, and hot sauce. Season with salt and pepper, stir to combine, and add the panko till the mixture holds together but is still moist. Add more panko if necessary.

3 Form 4 patties, and set aside for at least ten minutes before cooking; this lets the bread crumbs soak up all that liquid. Grill them as you would a beef burger or bake the patties in the oven at 350°F for 30 minutes.

4 BUILD YOUR BURGER: Bottom bun, lettuce, burger, tomato, onion, top bun. Add any of the traditional burger condiments—ketchup, mustard, mayo, relish, etc. Give your heart a little meat vacation, give the cows a day off, and then it's back to beef tomorrow!

MEDITERR-AIN'T MISBEHAVIN' BURGER

SEASON 2, EPISODE 9: BEEFSQUATCH

A nice thick slice of eggplant, topped with roasted chickpeas and a minty fresh tzatziki sauce! MAKES AT LEAST 4 "BURGERS"

---

1 large eggplant, sliced into
 ½-inch thick rounds

Salt

1 15-ounce can chickpeas,
 drained and rinsed

1 tablespoon olive oil

1 teaspoon salt

1 tablespoon paprika

1 teaspoon ground cumin

½ cucumber

½ cup plain Greek yogurt

2 teaspoons fresh lemon juice

2 teaspoons chopped fresh dill

1 teaspoon chopped fresh mint

4 buns

Arugula

---

1 Generously salt the eggplant slices on a baking rack or colander set over a bowl. Let sit for about 15 minutes to draw out the liquid, then flip and repeat. Discard the liquid and rinse the salt from the eggplant before proceeding.

2 Sauté the chickpeas in the olive oil with the salt, paprika, and cumin until lightly browned and toasty. Like when you had that great tan. You remember that time.

3 To make the tzatziki sauce, first peel, halve, and scoop out the seeds from the cucumber. Finely dice to yield about ⅓ cup and combine with the yogurt, lemon juice, dill, and mint in a small bowl. If it is too thick, add a teaspoon or two of water.

4 Grill, pan fry, or broil the eggplant in the oven until it starts to brown.

5 BUILD YOUR BURGER: Bottom bun, arugula, eggplant, a scoop of chickpeas, a heavy drizzle of tzatziki sauce, top bun.

TOP BUN

TZATZIKI SAUCE

CHICKPEAS

SLICED EGGPLANT

ARUGULA

BOTTOM BUN

ACKNOWLEDGMENTS

Making a TV show is hard. Making a book is even harder, it turns out. Making both at the same time is basically nuts. Below are the people who, despite knowing how unwise this whole enterprise was, signed on and made it happen.

First, hugest thanks to **Cole Bowden**, **Janelle Momary-Neely**, and **Carly Berezin Hartogsohn**. Cole worked in his kitchen, Janelle and Carly in their offices here at *Bob's Burgers*. And all three of them worked furiously to make this book happen while doing their *other, actual jobs*. (And doing them well.) Janelle moved mountains not just so this book might exist, but exist at its highest potential. Everyone in the world should have Janelle helping them accomplish their goals. Carly, working with **Jono Jarrett**, our fearless editor at Rizzoli, not only watch-dogged the schedule and workflow, but also shaped and guided the content. The words, the images, and the layout—Carly and Jono touched every square millimeter of every page and both covers, an impressive feat of left brain/right brain coordination. In addition to lending us his skills, we also want to thank Jono for his patience—nice folks here at *Bob's Burgers*, but we had zero book-writing experience when we took this on. That must have been fun for him.

Julie Fisher Haro, **Mike Olsen**, **Pete Truss**, and **Rachel Hastings** backed up Carly here at Bob's and we salute them as well.

We thank our culinary consultants: **Paul O'Connell** and **Aliza Miner**, who made the first, second, and third greatest sandwiches I've ever eaten. We knew they would be valuable, but we didn't know *how* valuable. They helped refine Cole's vision without diminishing its essential *Cole-ness*.

Giant thanks to our key artists: **Anthony Aguinaldo** and **Hector Reynoso**. Anthony designed all those deconstructed burgers that you probably want posters of, as well as character art and color. Hector designed most of the character art and the food props. And again, they did this while working on a television show that *also* demands their full attention and time. We thank **Bernard Derriman** and **Tony Gennaro** as well, for sketches, designs, notes, artistic guidance, and generally good attitude.

Even more great artists touched these pages: **Maggie Harbaugh**, **Damon Wong**, **Frank Forte**, **Ira Sherak**, **Daniel Lim**, **Anthony Imperato**, **Derek Schroeder**, **Young Chan Jeon**, **Kyung Shin**, **Ken Laramay**—we thank you.

We want to thank our *Bob's Burgers* writers, who generate, on average, ten thousand burgers of the day for every one that makes it to the board. They came up with every single pun in this punstival (that's a festival for puns), and then generously added their voices, jokes, and joke-like asides to the text: **Nora Smith**, **Wendy** and **Lizzie Molyneux**, **Dan Fybel**, **Jim Dauterive**, **Holly Schlesinger**, **Greg Thompson**, **Steven Davis**, **Kelvin Yu**, **Jon Schroeder**, and **Scott Jacobson**. **Rich Rinaldi**, **Mike Olsen**, **Mike Benner**, and **Kit Boss** all contributed burgers though not punch-up. We thank them heartily nonetheless. What's so great about punch-up, right? Why does everyone need to laugh so much?

And we thank our families. Holly, I promise no more cookbooks. (Unless this sells really well.)

THE BOB'S BURGERS BURGER BOOK

By Loren Bouchard
and the writers of Bob's Burgers
Recipes by Cole Bowden
Illustrations by Bento Box Entertainment
Design by Lynne Yeamans/Lync

© 2016 20th Television

For information address Hyperion Avenue, 77 West 66th Street,
New York, New York 10023.

First Hardcover Edition, March 2016
First Hyperion Avenue Edition, February 2021

10 9 8 7 6

ISBN 978-1-368-07106-2
Library of Congress Control Number: 2015946975
FAC-034274-24024
Printed in the United States of America

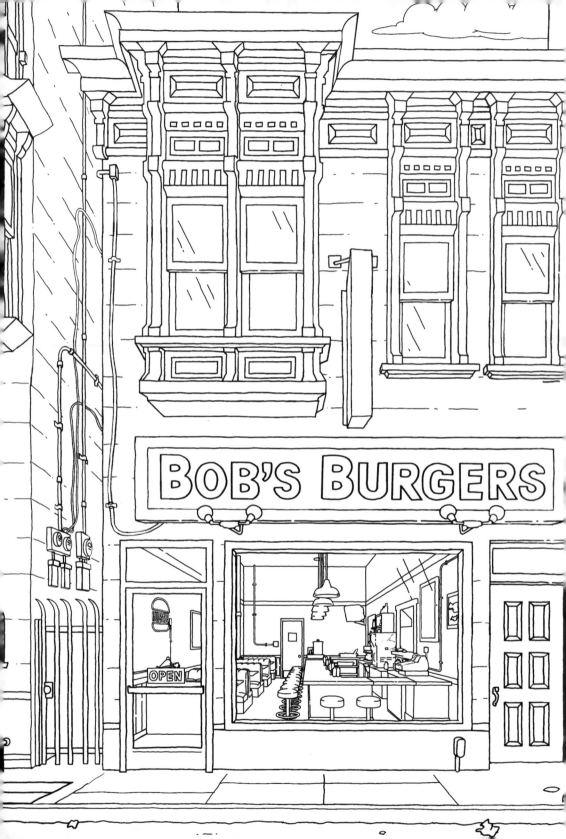